The media's watching Vault!
Here's a sampling of our coverage.

"Unflinching, fly-on-the-wall reports... No one gets past company propaganda to the nitty-gritty inside dope better than these guys."
— *Knight-Ridder newspapers*

"Best way to scope out potential employers...Vault.com has sharp insight into corporate culture and hiring practices."
— *Yahoo! Internet Life*

"Vault.com has become a de facto Internet outsourcer of the corporate grapevine."
— *Fortune*

"For those hoping to climb the ladder of success, [Vault.com's] insights are priceless."
— *Money.com*

D1714480

"Another killer app for the Internet."
— *New York Times*

"If only the company profiles on the top sites would list the 'real' information... Sites such as Vault.com do this, featuring insights and commentary from employees and industry analysts."
— *The Washington Post*

"A rich repository of information about the world of work."
— *Houston Chronicle*

VAULT
> the most trusted name in career information™

VAULT GUIDE TO CONQUERING CORPORATE AMERICA
FOR WOMEN AND MINORITIES

VAULT GUIDE TO CONQUERING CORPORATE AMERICA
FOR WOMEN AND MINORITIES

PATRICIA KAO, SUSAN TIEN
AND THE STAFF OF VAULT

Library of Congress Cataloging-in-Publication Data

Kao, Patricia.
Vault guide to conquering corporate America for women and minorities /Patricia Kao and
Susan Tien.– 1st ed.
    p. cm.
ISBN 1-58131-178-8 (pbk. : alk. paper)
  1. Vocational guidance for women. 2. Vocational guidance for minorities. 3. Diversity in
the workplace. 4. Women executives. 5. Minorities--Employment. I. Tien, Susan. II. Title.
HF5382.6.K36 2003
650.1'08--dc21

                                                                          2003007449

Printed in the United States of America

ACKNOWLEDGEMENTS

We would like to thank all of our friends and family for supporting this project with great enthusiasm. A special thanks to:

- Samer Hamadeh for supporting the original proposal;
- Marcy Lerner for providing great feedback at every turn;
- Janelle McGlothlin, Alan Tien, and Bill Cheng for taking the time to edit drafts;
- Sonya Xu for providing the legal discrimination section;
- All of our friends and family who contributed anecdotes to the book.

Susan would like to thank her parents, Alan and Mae-Ling Tien, Bill Cheng, and co-author Patty for their love and support.

Patty would like to thank her parents, Mary and Tim, brother Christopher, and best friend co-author Susan.

Vault would like to acknowledge the assistance and support of Matt Doull, Ahmad Al-Khaled, Lee Black, Eric Ober, Hollinger Ventures, Tekbanc, New York City Investment Fund, American Lawyer Media, Globix, Hoover's, Glenn Fischer, Mark Hernandez, Ravi Mhatre, Carter Weiss, Ken Cron, Ed Somekh, Isidore Mayrock, Zahi Khouri, Sana Sabbagh and other Vault investors. Many thanks to our loving families and friends.

**Deloitte
& Touche**

be there

P&G

"I can be me at P&G."

Diversity plays a lead role at Procter & Gamble. Everyone is bound by the same goal—to produce better ideas, superior service and outstanding products. Diversity is key to this goal. Our diversity covers a broad range of personal attributes and characteristics. We feel the resulting mixture of people, cultures, education, personalities and opportunities provides a richer environment for innovation, which leads to success in the global marketplace.

*Visit our website at **www.pg.com**.*

Table of Contents

Chapter 11: Troubleshooting Common Problems   131

Chapter 12: Maintaining Your Equilibrium   145

Chapter 13: Evaluating your Job/Moving On   153

FINAL ANALYSIS   159

APPENDIX   161

Imagine a place where
opportunities are endless

Hewitt

IT REALLY **iS** ALL ABOUT YOU.

We know, you've heard that before. But at INROADS® it's true. Apply for the Internship that gets you into America's top companies. You're a high achiever. Have good grades. And a burning desire to rock the corporate world. So why wait until you graduate? You can be there NOW.

INROADS Interns work for companies like **GE, Verizon, Lockheed Martin and other Fortune 500s.** Take the opportunity to lead and grow. Get training from executive mentors. Get the inside track to a great career and a great future. And get paid.

INROADS is listed by the Princeton Review as one of America's Top Ten Internships. So, if you've got what it takes, take the first step.

To apply online, visit us at **www.INROADS.org.**

The mission of INROADS is to develop and place

TALENTED MINORITY YOUTH *in business and industry and prepare them for corporate and community* **LEADERSHIP.**

INROADS®

Introduction

Every year, many new college and professional school grads get their first jobs as entry-level employees in Corporate America. The client service industries in particular – management consulting, investment banking, law and accounting – employ a new army of young worker bees every fall season. Lured by the opportunity to make a great deal of money and gain a broad education in the business world, recent grads often enter the corporate environment with no understanding of the written and unwritten rules of Corporate America to guide their behavior. They simply expect their new employers to train them completely.

We wrote this book for the benefit of those with little practical experience with the inner workings of the corporate world. The advice we offer comes from our personal experience and those of our friends and colleagues. We are presenting everything we wish we had known our first day on the job, but didn't. We had little exposure to the corporate world – our parents were academics, small business owners, and immigrants to boot. We scrambled to get up to speed, made a lot of painful mistakes doing it and envied our peers who seemed so much more comfortable in the same environment.

Women and minorities need to be particularly savvy in navigating the maze of office protocol and politics. The corporate world has historically been a heterosexual, white male playground. Women usually lack the prior experiences, role models and mentors to guide their climb up the corporate ladder. Minorities face those and additional obstacles. Often, new female and minority hires start their jobs ready to conquer the world, only to find their enthusiasm and confidence eroded as they face each additional pitfall. And no wonder. They see few successful survivors of their kind at the top of the ladder. In 2002, only 11 *Fortune* 1000 companies were led by women. Among *Fortune's* list of the "Best 50 Companies for Minorities," only 24 percent of officials and managers that the employers honored were actually minorities.

Most of the people we interviewed for anecdotes are like us: successful women or minorities who are about ten years into their corporate careers. We collected their stories of hard lessons learned, as well as great advice lucky ones received early on. We wanted to target this group of peers for advice for a number of reasons. They are close enough to their own first days to remember their earliest successes and failures, yet now have the distance and maturity to see the lessons learned. They have successfully ascended the corporate ladder, and now manage junior people who make the same mistakes. Their advice will help you confront the same or similar situations.

We want to demystify the path to early and consistent success in the corporate world. We outline basic tips on the management, organization and presentation of yourself and your work during the time you spend at the bottom of the corporate food chain. We help you identify and balance what's important to your employer versus what's important to you. Learn about actively managing your environment, minimizing your blind spots, and keeping your eyes on the prize – getting the great experience necessary to move onto something better, all the while maintaining your physical and emotional health!

Our simple objective is to prepare you to deal with as many potentially tricky situations as possible. Pick and choose the advice in this book that is relevant to your job and company. You'll be well on your way to conquering the corporate world!

This book will discuss:

- What to expect at your new company. We'll discuss different types of companies and show how the differences are reflected in your work environment and corporate culture, namely the rules governing your work community. Your ability to perceive and respect these rules will determine whether your colleagues think you are appropriately "professional" and, ultimately, "promotable."

- Basic skills to get yourself organized, disciplined and efficient in producing your work. We focus on the time management and organization skills you need to help you get on track immediately and keep you there.

- Key communication skills so you know how to communicate with your boss and your co-workers. We will teach you to maximize the impact of your written and verbal communications in a professional environment.

- Day-to-day skills covering phone etiquette, meetings and document creation. Throughout your career, you will find yourself performing the same basic tasks on a typical business day.

- How to get the most out of your evaluations. Read pointers on the dreaded evaluation process.

- How to manage your relationships with your boss, co-workers, peers and clients. Relationships will be critical to your professional efficiency, happiness and advancement.

- How to network and get mentors. You need a support group and a safety net to succeed in this job and future jobs. We discuss building and maintaining these relationships.

- How to maneuver around obstacles and pitfalls specific to women and minorities. We will focus on subtle and blatant discrimination and suggest solutions for preparing yourself.

- How to fix common problems and avoid them in the future. We give you tips on damage control when you make a mistake and on defusing tough situations.

- Maintaining your equilibrium. We will instruct you on how to stay physically and emotionally healthy, by balancing work and life.

Visit Vault at **www.vault.com** for insider company profiles, expert advice, career message boards, expert resume reviews, the Vault Job Board and more.

VAULT CAREER LIBRARY

3

Losing sleep over your job search?
Endlessly revising your resume?
Facing a work-related dilemma?

Super-charge your career with Vault's newest career tools: Resume Reviews, Resume Writing and Career Coaching.

Vault Resume Writing

On average, a hiring manager weeds through 120 resumes for a single job opening. Let our experts write your resume from scratch to make sure it stands out.

- Start with an e-mailed history and 1- to 2-hour phone discussion
- Vault experts will create a first draft
- After feedback and discussion, Vault experts will deliver a final draft, ready for submission

Vault Resume Review

- Submit your resume online
- Receive an in-depth e-mailed critique with suggestions on revisions within TWO BUSINESS DAYS

Vault Career Coach

Whether you are facing a major career change or dealing with a workplace dilemma, our experts can help you make the most educated decision via telephone counseling sessions.

- Sessions are 45-minutes over the telephone

For more information go to
www.vault.com/careercoach

VAULT
> the most trusted name in career information™

THE SCOOP

Corporate Culture:
The Written and Unwritten Rules of Companies

CHAPTER 2

Corporate culture is the name given to the mass of written and unwritten values, beliefs, traditions and rules of behavior that govern how things are done at any given company. Corporate culture is usually deeply rooted and taken for granted. Each company has its own corporate culture. Sometimes departments or groups within a company will have distinct cultures. The larger the company is, the more calcified its company culture is likely to be.

Should you care about corporate culture? Absolutely. Corporate culture influences how employees are valued, compensated and promoted, what behavior is rewarded, who fits in and who doesn't. New employees are often hired (or not hired) on the basis of their "fit" with corporate culture.

Assessing your personal fit with a prospective employer's corporate culture is very important. The better you fit with the culture, the happier your tenure at the company will be. The culture will set the hours you work, the tone of your work environment, the formality of your appearance, how you interact with managers, co-workers and clients, and how you manage your career path. In addition, company culture very often controls how comfortable women and minorities will be at any given firm.

Before you start

Try to get a feel for the corporate culture of a company as early as possible – preferably before your first interview! Do some research on the Web. Read the company's web site and see if it has a mission statement, or if it avows certain policies. Check out how many women and minorities the firm has in its senior management. If possible, talk to current employees at the firm about what it's like to work there. Getting the inside scoop from actual employees is always best, as what a company promotes in its mission statement and press releases can often differ from reality. (It's also the only way to get information about firms that lack informative web sites or lots of press coverage.)

Once you start at a company, learn the rules of the system as quickly as possible, not only to avoid mistakes, but to thrive in your job. Read up on policies. Note the frequency, level of detail and tone of the news communicated at team, department and company-wide meetings. Ask your

Visit Vault at **www.vault.com** for insider company profiles, expert advice, career message boards, expert resume reviews, the Vault Job Board and more.

VAULT CAREER LIBRARY

7

more experienced peers what kind of behavior is expected and what is not allowed. Observe interactions to get a sense of real power dynamics.

As you learn the rules, both written and unwritten, FOLLOW them! As a newcomer, some company norms may seen odd to you. But as a new hire in an entry-level position, you are not in a position to criticize, change or test the rules, yet. Your performance will be evaluated, in part, by how well you follow established policy and fit into the existing culture.

Hierarchy

Companies handle power differently. This structure will affect your role in the company, not just as you start but as you build a career. Some companies are very hierarchical. The chain of command is crystal clear, and bypassing that chain is unacceptable. For example, in law firms, a first-year associate turns in work for review by a senior associate, who in turn gives it to the partner before the work product is given to the client. Process is just as important as performance. Even if employees produce results, they can still be poorly reviewed, even fired, for not following proper company procedure.

Other companies are more meritocratic. They place greater emphasis on performance and work quality. The hierarchy is much flatter. For example, you may be able to go over your boss' head without immediate repercussions. This kind of company is more likely to reward mavericks. They also tend to foster employees with "unofficial" power.

IMPORTANT: In either type of company, find out what the management style is, and do not test the system your first year there.

Your Performance

So you've landed the position, but how are you supposed to know whether you are doing a good job? There may or may not be clear standards of expected performance at your company. Some companies have strict guidelines for performance. Employees are reviewed on a regular basis and must meet the standards of their current position within a certain period of time in order to advance to the next level of pay or responsibility. Those who don't make the grade are weeded out. This is called an "up or out" system. Other companies have less rigid ways to grade performance. Such companies may allow more latitude for employees, especially if they are well-liked or politically connected, but it also means that employees may not have any warning that their performance is not considered up to snuff. (Smaller companies and companies in more "creative" industries, such as advertising and publishing, tend to have less formal review systems, depending on corporate culture.)

What happens if you do well? If you're lucky, you may get a raise or even a promotion. The most likely immediate consequence of strong performance, however, is that you will get more work to do. Managers typically care about results and not the equity of workloads. That's why you sometimes hear strong performers complain that there's no real benefit to doing an outstanding job. That's exactly the wrong attitude. Don't complain about getting extra work – assuming that it's real work and not routine administrative work. (We'll discuss the common issue of women getting socked with doing administrative duties outside the scope of their position later.) Extra experience and education always pay off in the long run.

Hours

Your company's culture may influence the hours you are expected to work, though the ultimate arbiter of your schedule will be your manager. Some environments are result-oriented. Once you have finished your work for the day, you can go home. If you have a class to take or an appointment, you are able to come in late one day and work late the next – just as long as you get your work done. In other environments, you are expected to be in the office between set hours regardless of how busy you are. Even if you have finished all of your work and have no new projects, you will be expected to sit at your desk and pretend to be busy. (This practice of feigning work is also called "face time.") If you're in a face time-oriented environment, leaving early may make you stand out in a bad way. Don't be surprised if co-workers make snide comments to your face, such as, "Only working a half-day?"

Companies purposely hire young grads because they know grads will work very hard to get some good experience on their blank resumes. Prepare to work at least 50 hours a week on average. Expect to work weekends and late nights regularly, including the occasional all-nighter, especially during your first two years when you are earning your stripes. Client service companies like investment banks, accounting firms, management consulting firms and law firms will expect even longer hours. And then there are law firms and investment banks that are notorious for 100-hour-plus workweeks, involving one or more nights spent at the office. Expect to work hard no matter what.

Visit Vault at **www.vault.com** for insider company profiles, expert advice, career message boards, expert resume reviews, the Vault Job Board and more.

V∧ULT CAREER LIBRARY

9

> **TIP:** As a rule, try to follow your manager's work hours if he works a lot, but don't follow your manager's work hours if he is prone to running out in the middle of the day for a few hours. If your manager regularly arrives at the office at 6 a.m. and you get in early as well, he will think of you as a hard worker. You might even get to schmooze your boss more easily at a time when few other employees are in the office. However, just because your boss takes two-hour lunches does not mean that it's OK for you to do the same!

While you should plan to have a life outside of work, be prepared to experience the disappointment of canceling social plans and even the occasional vacation. Plan realistically, and don't be too optimistic about making frequent extracurricular plans in the middle of an important project.

What time you start work and how long you stay can vary greatly based on your company, your department or team, and your boss. Different teams within one company can work very different hours. One manager may expect his team to work ten hours a day, while another manager may expect her team to work 12 hours a day. One department head may expect the workday to start at 8 a.m., while another department head turns a blind eye when employees straggle in around 10 a.m. Sometimes these differences are driven by the manager's personal lifestyle; for example, someone with kids may need to start early and end early. You may also be unfortunate enough to have a boss with poor time management skills who routinely gives you work at the last minute.

IMPORTANT: Whether your day is driven by your manager's personal preferences or external business factors, follow the expected schedule when you are at the bottom of the corporate ladder. You are paid to be available for your managers and for your clients when they want you to be available. While it's OK if you arrive late once in a while, your reliability will be questioned if you violate the rules regularly.

Remember that you don't get credit for working when people are not around to see you. You may feel justified for coming into work an hour later than the rest of your team because you're planning to stay late or you worked a couple of hours at home over the weekend. But here's a sad fact: no one will care that you worked overtime the day or weekend beforehand. All they'll see is that they're in the office and you're not. (Psychologically, it seems easier for others to understand if you get into work early and need to leave early.) In short, unless you have a written arrangement with your boss, don't take a job if you cannot conform to its schedule.

Women, Minorities and Office Culture

Every year, *Fortune* publishes a list of the most desirable companies for minorities. *Fortune*'s criteria include the diversity of the workforce and senior management, as well as the presence of programs to encourage greater workforce diversity. *Working Mother* also publishes an annual list of the best companies for working mothers. Some companies strive to cultivate a positive relationship with women and minorities, and some avoid the issue. It is worth your time to research your employer's track record on hiring and promoting women and minorities before you accept a position.

Office Manners

No matter the company or the culture, the same good manners you were taught by your mother apply to your office environment, too.

- Treat others with the same respect you expect from them.

- Do not chew with your mouth open, and do not talk with your mouth full. You will be eating many meals with your co-workers and clients. Make sure you chew your food slowly and with your mouth shut. If you don't, you will gross people out and diminish your professional impression, but no one will know how to tell you. Don't eat while you're on the phone, either. People can tell.

- Do not interrupt people while they are talking. Let them finish their sentences, even if you don't agree with what they are saying!

- Listen carefully. People will respond to you much more positively if they feel you are attentive. Acknowledge what they are saying with direct eye contact, nods, facial expressions and other subtle reactions.

- Don't yell. Yelling at someone in the office is unprofessional and mean. There is always a way to express anger, frustration or disappointment in a calm voice.

- Observe the rules of grammar. Speak correctly.

- Don't swear… unless you are in a macho, testosterone-fueled business, where swearing may not only be accepted but expected in order to be "one of the guys." Even if you swear in front of your team in order to fit in,

Visit Vault at **www.vault.com** for insider company profiles, expert advice, career message boards, expert resume reviews, the Vault Job Board and more.

VAULT CAREER LIBRARY   **11**

refrain from profanity and coarse language in front of other departments, superiors or clients.

- Do not run through the halls. Unless you are about to miss a FedEx deadline, there is no reason to run, and it is dangerous and disruptive. You could trip and fall, plow into someone stepping out of an office, or just really anger the senior executives in the conference room when you go pounding past.

Sharing Space

Sharing space with your office mates can be difficult. You may be sharing an office with co-workers, or sitting in a cubicle inches away from your neighbors. Here are some tips on making the close quarters work for you:

- Keep your space neat. Not only will you avoid spilling over into other people's space, it also will make it easier for people to find files off your desk without having to ransack the place.

- Make your space cozy with plants, pictures and other personal items.

- If you eat food at your desk, throw away the garbage in the kitchen so you don't subject co-workers in your area to the smell of leftovers all day.

- Keep your voice down when talking on the phone. It maintains your privacy and spares your neighbors the disruption.

- Do not comment on other people's conversations or laugh at other people's jokes when they are talking on the phone, even if it is impossible not to overhear. Cubicle protocol is to pretend you don't hear each other.

- Listen to music at a low volume or with headphones. It will keep you from getting distracted by the noise around you.

- If you have to make an important phone call or conduct an important meeting, use a conference room or unused office so you are not distracted.

- Keep confidential work materials confidential. Be careful about what documents you leave up on your computer screen or sitting on your desk, printer or fax machine, especially a resume! Also, be careful about working on personal documents on a shared network drive.

- Do not keep anything of personal value out in the open. Your co-workers may be honest, but you probably don't realize how many outside people traipse through your office when you are not around (e.g., visitors, messengers, janitors).

- Do not take things from other people or open any of their drawers or files without permission. If you need to borrow a file or a stapler from a co-worker, ask their permission first. If they are not around, leave them a post-it note on their chair, desk or computer screen to let them know what you borrowed. Either way, return the item as soon as possible.

Professional Appearance

Every company has a level of professional dress that is expected of its employees. Regardless of the quality of your work, people will question your business judgment if you have poor judgment in attire. Furthermore, the appropriateness of your dress will directly affect the amount of face time your manager will give you in front of superiors and clients, and therefore affects your career development. Here's how to make sure you're dressed appropriately:

- Dress slightly more formally than your peers. Do not be the most casually dressed person in the room.

- Err on the side of being overdressed around superiors and clients. If the dress code in your office becomes more formal with seniority, you should dress for the level to which you aspire. (That is, if managers wear suits, but your peers dress business casual, wear a suit once in while to demonstrate your aspirations.) But if the office dress code becomes less formal with seniority, conform to the formality of your level. Just because your CEO wears jeans and sneakers doesn't mean you have earned the right to dress similarly.

- Be careful at company events, even if they are cocktail events or evening parties. Women are especially prone to err in this area. Don't see an office party as an excuse to wear the latest in iridescent eye shadow and trendy low-cut gowns. To be blunt, you shouldn't look too sexy. It's best to rely on the standard little black dress. (But make sure it's not too little!)

- If others can identify what makeup you're wearing, you're wearing too much. Keep it subdued.

- Dress conservatively for nonwork functions you know colleagues are attending. Unfortunately, even an impression you make in your free time outside of the office can follow you into the office on Monday morning.

Visit Vault at **www.vault.com** for insider company profiles, expert advice, career message boards, expert resume reviews, the Vault Job Board and more.

V/\ULT CAREER LIBRARY

13

- What does "business casual" mean? Generally, it looks like the nicer stuff in Banana Republic. For men, it means khakis or slacks, button-down oxford or polo shirts, sweaters or sports jackets, belt, socks, leather shoes. For women, it means a blouse and a skirt or a dress. No jeans, shorts, tank-tops, T-shirts or flip-flops. Don't assume brand name designers or expensive price tags make clothes appropriate for office wear. One stylish law associate wore men's open-heel sandals to work one day. When his manager told him they were too casual for the office, he replied, "But they're Gucci!"

- Here's a simple way to tell whether your skirt is too short. Your skirt should never be more than a handswidth above your knee. Just stand up and wrap your hand around your leg just above the knee. If your skirt does not touch your hand, it is too short.

- What does "casual Friday" mean? For the West Coast, it means you can wear jeans (still avoid flip-flops, shorts and tank tops). In the Midwest and East Coast, jeans are still generally off limits, but you can wear the more casual versions of khakis, or sometimes corduroys in the winter.

- Even if you dress casually at the office, always keep appropriate business clothes available in case a client meeting suddenly arises. Don't let yourself be excluded from an important meeting because you didn't wear the appropriate clothes to work. In an emergency, you can run out and buy appropriate dress.

- If you are traveling to your company office or a client in a different region, check up on the weather and local dress code before you go.

- Try not to make your hair too memorable. Men should note the styles of managers and clients. Generally speaking, businessmen part their hair on the side, not down the middle. A balding man should keep his hair trimmed very short for the most professional look. Facial hair is usually acceptable as long as it is clean and well-kept, but if you can bear to lose the goatee, it's even better to be clean-shaven.

Women who wear their hair longer than shoulder length should keep it well groomed. While it's unfair, curly hair can look messy and unprofessional if it is too long. If you do have long curly hair, consider pulling it back into a bun or braid during the day. Pigtails are never OK in Corporate America. African-American women can wear neat braids or short natural styles; elaborate colored extensions and unruly dreads should be avoided.

The Importance of Looking Professional
Wall Street Executive

I went straight through college into graduate school. My first summer internship in graduate school was on Wall Street. I had never worked in any building taller than five stories, let alone in a position that required wearing a suit and tie. During my human resources orientation, I took subtle note that the HR person wrote down the color of my suit. I merely took it as a passing formality.

Weeks went by, and I was solidly enjoying my internship, but what I deemed as strange comments started to appear. My shoes were coming apart, so I simply applied some rubber cement to seal the base together. My boss commented, "You might want to get a new pair of shoes; people notice these things." I wasn't quite sure if he was kidding or not and dismissed his comment. Someone a week later asked me if I had any nice ties. Again, I dismissed the comment. I thought it was a joke.

Finally came the clincher. A fellow associate took me aside and read me the sartorial riot act. He told me that he had been instructed to speak to me regarding my attire. I immediately became defensive, as I was not chummy with this pompous guy, but a sixth sense told me to listen, so I did. He bought me an issue of GQ, and we went through it. While the goal was not to look like a GQ model, it became apparent that I needed to do a little more for my wardrobe. I only had two suits (both took a serious workout that summer), two pairs of shoes (one of which was rubber soled), and three white shirts, which I washed and ironed myself. He gave me several tips:

1. Buy a good suit. I bought two, one virgin wool navy blue and one worsted wool gray pinstripe suit, both cuffed 1.25 inches at the bottom (Hickey Freeman and Zegna). They actually felt nicer.

2. Buy a good pair of leather "captoe" shoes and a matching leather belt. Keep them shined. I had never shined my dusty loafers and promptly got rid of my rubber-soled shoes.

3. Buy combed cotton undershirts. They felt great – a big difference from Hanes.

4. Buy collar stays to keep your collars straight.

5. Stop ironing your shirts. Buy ten and send them to the cleaners. Always get them on a hanger and lightly starched. You can buy

Visit Vault at www.vault.com for insider company profiles, expert advice, career message boards, expert resume reviews, the Vault Job Board and more.

VAULT CAREER LIBRARY   15

white shirts or blue shirts. You can't buy cuffed shirts until you're a VP.

6. Socks are an extension of pant color. Get matching ones.

7. Get some good ties and tie in a 4-in-hand-knot, with a dimple. I never thought I would spend more than $30 on a tie, but I did.

While I didn't do everything that he said, I did realize that I needed to spend money here, and I did. Bottom line: this investment paid off, and folks commented on the improvements. My attire became a nonissue there and in subsequent jobs. As a matter of fact, I found that I enjoyed dressing well, and co-workers actually complimented me on my style.

I never really liked the guy and thought the "clothing intervention" was demeaning. But I am thankful for the message, and that someone took the time to say something to me.

Now I can wear cufflink shirts!

Hygiene

You will spend much of your professional life in small spaces – conference rooms, offices, cubicles, elevators – working side by side with colleagues and clients and breathing recycled air. There's no polite way to tell you that you don't smell good, so people will talk behind your back. At one consulting company, an employee did not bathe frequently; people said they could tell how many days ago she had showered last by how far down the hall her odor wafted. It took months before anyone told her of the problem. Make sure you:

- Take a shower daily and always wear deodorant. This routine is the norm in corporate environments and is non-negotiable.

- Avoid perfume and cologne. No matter how much you like your perfume or cologne, and no matter how lightly you apply it, leave it for the weekend. You don't know who will be allergic or find the smell noxious.

- Avoid smoking. Companies typically relegate smokers to a cramped outdoor spot. If you smoke, try to minimize smoke breaks during the day to avoid having the smell cling to your clothes and breath. If you must smoke during the day, be careful to air out your clothes and chew gum before you head back inside the office.

Professional Demeanor

Though you'll spend as much or more time with your co-workers as you will with family and friends, remember that they are not your family. To thrive in the corporate world, you'll need to keep your game face on at all times.

DO...

- **Exude calm and confidence.** Crises are inevitable. When things go bad, you should strive to be remembered as the calm person in the room. Think about it – would you rather have a teammate who can push through a crisis or one who freaks out? (Women are often stereotyped as being overly emotional, so keeping calm is even more important for them.)

Maintain Your Cool to Be a Leader
Lisa Strick, Marketing Executive

I have learned the difficult lesson that strong commitment and passion for your work can cause you to appear emotional. Unfortunately, most people are uncomfortable with emotions and tend not to listen to a message when it is presented in an expressive style. In general, people don't want to be worried or upset and tend to have more confidence in those that appear more aloof. It makes sense. Just imagine that a ship is sinking – who would you appoint as the leader to save the people, the emotional or the calm person? The key to remember: always be calm, cool and collected in a work environment. If you have to report a crisis or bad news to your co-workers or to a superior, maintain a positive attitude and keep your cool.

Visit Vault at **www.vault.com** for insider company profiles, expert advice, career message boards, expert resume reviews, the Vault Job Board and more.

VAULT CAREER LIBRARY   17

Keep a Level Head in a Stressful Situation

Adriel G. Lares, Director of Finance at 3PARdata Inc.

In my previous life as an investment banking analyst, I was in Baltimore on a roadshow for a high profile technology IPO. While in the shower at 5 a.m., I ran through all of the objectives for the day. After Baltimore we were driving to DC, to have a meeting and then flying out to Europe. Then it hit me. Where was my passport? I mentally scanned my garment bag, satchel, folders, pants, everything. I mentally traced it back through all of the cities that we had hit and ultimately back to my dresser drawer in California.

Immediately, I started thinking of alternatives. Can I use something else instead? No. You need a passport. Can I stop by a consulate and get an emergency one? No time. Our flight leaves at 7 p.m. and I have meetings all day. I can't send the clients by themselves to Europe on a plane with no accompaniment. My managing director was going to kill me!

At this point I began to panic. I told myself that there was a solution. I just didn't know what it was yet. I had to be downstairs by 6:45 a.m. to meet the client executives for our first meeting of the day. I needed to figure this out in the next hour. Then I remembered hearing something on TV about a same day service provided by FedEx. I called them to ask about the details. You lose time as you travel east, but it can be done. An item picked up by 8 a.m. can be delivered between 5 p.m. and 6 p.m. on the East Coast.

So, I had to get my passport (if it even was in my dresser drawer) from my home to the office for FedEx pickup. I frantically called my roommates for thirty minutes (it was about 2:30 a.m. Pacific time) until some poor sap picked up the phone, and then took another ten minutes trying to wake him up and explain the situation. I finally convinced one of them to find my passport (fortunately, it was where I thought it was), drive to the office, package it up and leave it outside for pickup.

I called FedEx and told them where to pick it up, and then they asked me where I wanted it delivered. Delivered? Where was I going to be that they could deliver it? I told them to deliver it to the Dulles Marriott. I had no idea if there was a Marriott at Dulles airport but I figured I had a good chance. With FedEx on the phone I called information on my cell, and found that there was one. I communicated the delivery address and then I was off.

Amazingly enough, I didn't even stress out about it because I was dealing with all of the details of that day's roadshow. It wasn't until about 4:30 p.m. when we were driving to the airport that a sinking feeling came over me. What if the FedEx guy couldn't find the package? What if it didn't arrive in time before I had to be at the airport for the early international check in? What if...?

I got the clients to the airport and sat them down for a quick bite to eat. It was 5 p.m. We needed to be ready to go around 6 p.m. I told them I needed to run an errand and that I would be back soon. I ran and took a cab to the Marriott. Thankfully, it was on the airport premises.

I don't know why I checked in, but I did and went to the room and laid down on the bed and prayed. Fifteen minutes later the phone rang: "Mr. Lares? We have a package down here for you."

I ran downstairs and picked up my passport. I got back by 5:30 p.m. and subsequently boarded the plane without anyone knowing that anything was amiss.

My lesson: remember your passport! And when your world has gone to hell in a handbasket, calm down and make a plan. Usually, there is a solution.

- **Go the extra mile as early as possible.** What separates you from any other newcomer at your company? If you simply do an adequate job, few people will remember you. If you do a superior job early on, your co-workers will think of you as a star and be much more forgiving of any later lapses.

  IMPORTANT: Distinguish between volunteering for good opportunities to shine versus tedious or futile missions. There will be opportunities for you to volunteer for different administrative committees in your office. If the committee is convening to plan a big event or execute a structural transition, the extra duties on top of your normal job are worth the chance to work with senior executives or colleagues from other departments you don't usually meet. But if the need is strictly administrative with lots of work and no glory, it may not be worth your time to participate. Your good work moving files over the weekend will be quickly forgotten.

Visit Vault at **www.vault.com** for insider company profiles, expert advice, career message boards, expert resume reviews, the Vault Job Board and more.

VAULT CAREER LIBRARY

19

In particular, do not volunteer for futile missions with lots of obstacles. The high risk of failure is not worth the small chance to be a hero. Once, a Wall Street analyst offered to hand deliver a bid proposal due at a specific hour in New Jersey. The bid was finished late, and traffic between New York and New Jersey prevented the guy from delivering the package on time. He was blamed by his department for disqualifying them from the deal, and wasting all of their work on the proposal. There was no reason for an analyst to deliver the bid in the first place; a courier would have been the obvious solution. Instead, the analyst created an opportunity to fail, and did.

Earn Your Reputation Early in Your Job
Software developer

It was probably two or three months into my first job after college when I pulled my one, and only, all-nighter at work. Though I wasn't too happy about it at the time (and certainly wouldn't do it again these days), it was great timing.

On the one hand, I wasn't at a company where all-nighters were the norm, so I wasn't worried about setting myself up as the guy who gets slammed with the all-nighters. On the flip side, my willingness to put in the hours when needed was certainly recognized. I became known as somebody who was committed and dependable, and as a result, I was given more responsibility and more interesting work very rapidly.

In addition, going the extra mile early helped me "bank some points" that I could cash in later – you'll always make a first impression, so it's better to make a good one with some early flexibility and hard work. And that hard work paid off financially with a nice bonus that holiday – something that my peers did not receive.

Earn Your Reputation
Janelle McGlothlin, former market analyst

We were having some issues with an FDA approval of an indication for a product in the medical environment. My boss volunteered me to help. I had to do a massive bibliography search and create an indexed reference of all the related studies.

We were scrambling to get the index out one night and ended up missing the FedEx drop-off in our building. Having been a procrastinator all my life, I knew the last possible drop-off was at the airport. I volunteered to drive it down there.

The next week, I had a letter on my desk from the president of the company thanking me for my extra efforts.

- **Maintain focus.** In the midst of a project crisis, looming deadline, or late hour, it is easy to cut corners and lower your standards of scrutiny. These stressful moments are exactly when you should triple-check your work to make sure nothing falls through the cracks. If you screw up, "I was stressed out" won't cut it as an excuse.

- **Be positive.** Attitude is everything. You make a choice to have a good attitude or a bad attitude. Your choice will affect your professionalism, your colleagues' work environment and your career development. Having a bad attitude about a situation you can't or won't change wastes your energy and negatively impacts your personal life and emotional health.

Maintain a Positive Attitude
Sucharita Mulpuru, former Disney analyst

Patience and attitude are often the most important things you can contribute. When I started my first job, I inherited a project to create some marketing materials that had been in the works with the two predecessors before me. My attitude was that I was going to work as hard as I could and be the person to bring the project to closure. I was going to accomplish something where others had failed.

Visit Vault at **www.vault.com** for insider company profiles, expert advice, career message boards, expert resume reviews, the Vault Job Board and more.

VAULT CAREER LIBRARY   21

> After about sixteen rounds of drafts that went back and forth over several months, with my manager always reluctant to "pull the trigger," I realized that it wasn't the fault of the two people before me that it had never been finished. My manager was unwilling to finish it – which had nothing to do with my wanting to get it done.
>
> I encountered countless projects like this in the years after my first job. The best advice is just to smile and keep delivering what the boss asks each time until he figures out what he wants.

- **Maintain a sense of humor.** A sense of humor will be your best resource for many situations. Whether you are working late, caught in an uncomfortable situation or trying to be memorable when networking with senior executives, a sense of humor is absolutely essential for defusing a tense moment, releasing stress and generally being a likable person. Your team will appreciate someone who can laugh at 4 a.m. when the copier jams for the tenth time and you still have five reports to reproduce. But don't go overboard by telling inappropriate jokes or playing annoying pranks.

- **Be accountable.** Take full ownership of your work. If you are assigned a project, be prepared to be responsible for the successes and the failures. Don't pass the buck. Nobody – clients, managers, teammates, peers, subordinates – will like or respect you if you do. Always share credit publicly for successes, and never deflect blame on others for failures.

- **Be humble.** If you consistently deliver top quality work, you will get the kudos you deserve without resorting to self-promotion. Sharing the credit will win you loyalty points with both your co-workers and your superiors.

Don't Showboat

Sharyn Ober-Hyatt, Director of Training, House of Blues Entertainment Inc.

My first boss and my mentor taught me two very important lessons:

1. Don't take credit for anything. Give the credit to others. No project is done in a vacuum, even if you are the lead on it.

2. Don't showboat. It's natural to want to be noticed at work, but proving yourself may be confused with grandstanding. No one likes a showoff.

I was working as a national service training manager for California Pizza Kitchen when my boss asked me to come with her to present new service training ideas to the president of the company.

The president asked whether we could reduce the number of days of the training program. My boss said that to maintain the integrity of the program, we needed that number of days. He then turned to me and asked the same question. I wanted to impress him so I said, "I believe we can reduce this program by at least three days."

Afterwards my boss wasn't very happy with me, and let me know that by undermining her in the meeting, I also made myself look bad. How were we going to reduce the training program? What impact would it have on the company? Would we be able to maintain our standards if we did reduce it? These were all questions I hadn't bothered to ask myself or her before blurting out an answer I thought the president wanted to hear.

Later I had to go back to him and let him know I was wrong. It was a tough lesson but one I will never forget.

DON'T...

- **Harbor a grudge.** It is extremely unlikely that the person you are holding the grudge against is dwelling on the same issue, so you're hurting yourself for no reason. Under no circumstances should you hold a grudge on behalf of someone else!

- **Lose your temper.** Unless you are a senior executive, there's really no way you can get away with throwing a tantrum or yelling at someone. You may get a reputation as an "angry" person, and if you lose your temper with a client, you might even be fired.

Visit Vault at **www.vault.com** for insider company profiles, expert advice, career message boards, expert resume reviews, the Vault Job Board and more.

VAULT CAREER LIBRARY   23

- **Reveal your insecurities.** You don't have to be great at everything at work. As long as you can get your work done, nobody needs to know what you think your weak areas are.

- **Complain excessively.** Change your situation or accept it. A little venting here and there in strict confidence to close friends is normal, but complaining openly and excessively seriously detracts from your focus and productivity, and produces bad results with:

    – Your colleagues. If your colleagues disagree or find you annoying, they will either complain about you to your manager or just start to avoid you. Even if they agree and chime in, you will fuel each other's negativity.

    – Your manager. The first few times you complain to your manager, your manager will most likely try to accommodate you. However, if you consistently complain, your manager will probably write you off as a troublemaker. This reaction is especially true if you are complaining about the manager herself!

Hide Your Frustration If Your Manager Wastes Your Time
Former management consultant

I had just completed several back-to-back 100-hour workweeks. As we progressed through our discussion in our next team meeting, I started to realize that the model I had built for 20 hours over the weekend would not be used. My manager had once again provided direction that led our team astray.

My face, apparently, revealed my frustration. I got an e-mail from the senior partner immediately following the meeting to ask if I was OK. Although I appreciated his concern, I also realized that I would need to do a better job of controlling my feelings, no matter how upset or frustrated I was.

I definitely developed a better game face over time. But there always will be moments when I struggle to pretend that things don't bother me.

Keep a Stiff Upper Lip

Victor Hwang, former corporate lawyer, current COO LARTA (a nonprofit think tank)

Law firm interviews typically involve going to lunch with lawyers at the firm, partly to see how you relate socially. I went to a law firm interview in Austin, feeling particularly sick from eating some nasty crab cakes the night before. At lunch, I politely refused to order anything other than a light salad, sure that I was on the verge of throwing up.

Lo and behold, after I swallowed my first crouton, I felt the urge and quickly excused myself to go to the bathroom. I vomited. A lot. Upon my return to the table, I must have appeared sweaty, exhausted, and somewhat green, because the three attorneys hosting my lunch were immediately sympathetic and kept asking how I was feeling. I kept my composure and just said that I was fine. Upon returning to the firm, I continued with my in-office interviews. Apparently, word had already spread about my reverse lunch, and people were joking with me about being the "walking wounded."

At the end of the visit, the managing partner offered me a summer job on the spot! The gist of what he said was that everyone was impressed with my composure in the face of adversity.

Office Chatter

Do not view office chitchat as wasted time! Small talk generates immeasurable goodwill. Make small talk with your colleagues around the office, even those who you don't personally like. Talk about their family, movies, TV shows, weather, weekend plans or sports events. People will actually notice who you greet and who you don't. Always greet assistants. They will talk behind your back if you ignore them, and may even badmouth you to their superiors.

Minimize gossiping about colleagues. Everyone enjoys a little gossip here and there about someone's new haircut, boring presentation, or sudden demotion. But for the most part, it's a good idea to save gossip for your personal life. If you must partake in office gossip, it is safer to listen to it than to pass it on. If you do indulge in spreading gossip, choose only your most trusted friends in the office. It's also possible that your boss may be interested in hearing office gossip and see you as a valued conduit. (If you

Visit Vault at www.vault.com for insider company profiles, expert advice, career message boards, expert resume reviews, the Vault Job Board and more.

VAULT CAREER LIBRARY   25

do gossip, it's better to spread positive or neutral gossip instead of negative or overly personal gossip.)

Adopt the business vernacular in your office if you want to fit in more quickly. Make sure you learn all the acronyms and lingo your colleagues use. Business vernacular and slang include sports analogies (e.g., "go the extra mile," "tee off the meeting," "take it over the finish line," etc.) and business or tech buzzwords ("incentivize," "innovate," "leverage," "interface," "bandwidth," "download," "platform," etc.). If you opt to use such vocabulary, make sure you are using it correctly. Also, don't use office lingo when you are talking to your family, friends or peers outside of the office.

Your Opinion

Prove yourself as a valuable team member before you reveal your personal opinions, politics and interests. You only have one chance to make a first impression. Don't let that first impression be skewed because you have been talking about subjects unrelated to your professional ability. ("Mary? You can't take what she says seriously. She's a tree hugger.")

Corporate America is quite conservative. Chances are, your firm is not a hotbed of liberalism. Susan and her co-workers were discussing the amount of taxes they had to pay from their first paycheck. When she said, "Yeah, the taxes are heavy, but I think we can afford it compared to the rest of the country," she was accused of being a communist!

Be Judged by Your Work, Not Your Politics
Lauren Weber, reporter for Reuters News Service

I've identified myself as a feminist since I was twelve years old. I started shaving my legs when I was fourteen and then stopped when I was fifteen because I saw no good reason to put in all that effort – it's a purely social convention with no utilitarian value whatever. My hairy legs were validated a few years later when I attended a very progressive liberal arts college with a strong feminist orientation – hardly anyone shaved their legs. I never reconsidered my position and none of the men I dated ever objected – it was a nonissue.

I worked in nonprofit organizations until I was 29, but then chose to pursue business journalism. After my first year in journalism school, I took an internship with *American Banker*, a daily newspaper serving – that's right – bankers. Though the office dress policy was casual, I started to think more about the impression I wanted to create. I didn't want my editors or my sources to recoil in horror if they caught a glimpse of my legs. To be sure, anyone who'd react like that is probably not someone I'd befriend. But this wasn't about friendship. This was about doing my job, and doing it as well as I could. And that meant relating to people professionally and ensuring that they'd relate to me professionally.

So after a little soul-searching, I decided it was time to say goodbye to my hirsute self and welcome my hairless-like-a-baby-rat self. I'm basically at peace with this change, since it's a superficial one and not a fundamental reordering of my political or social views. It's skin-deep. I don't pay much attention to my legs in winter, but come summer, I start it up pretty regularly. I'm sure I'll stick with this until I win a Pulitzer Prize and can then stop worrying about people not taking me seriously!

Office Ethics

Don't abuse perks, even if your company is abusing you. Today, companies need to project a squeaky-clean image. Your company will not hesitate to fire you if you threaten that image. As a result, it's always better to take the moral high ground. If you are ever terminated for ethical reasons, the incident will dog you for the rest of your professional life with every reference check for every new job. Nothing will sink your career faster than allegations of moral turpitude. It is not worth the "supplemental compensation."

A consulting analyst who produced top quality work was fired for his greed. He was intent on "sticking it to the company" and getting as much value as possible from the office to compensate for the late hours he consistently worked. When he was working late, he would expense two dinners and save one to eat on the weekend. He expensed a portable CD player, justifying it in his own mind as a travel accessory. His four years of great work were overshadowed by his poor judgment, and he left on bad terms with the partners.

The slippery slope of office abuses to avoid:

- Don't abuse your expense account. You will probably be given travel and entertainment guidelines. Observe them. If you don't, you may be stuck paying the difference later, or face a reprimand. If everyone is abusing the

Visit Vault at **www.vault.com** for insider company profiles, expert advice, career message boards, expert resume reviews, the Vault Job Board and more.

VAULT CAREER LIBRARY

27

system, don't volunteer your credit card to foot the bill. Every once in a while, the person who submits an egregious bill is stuck paying it.

- Don't fake anything. Don't fake an illness to get a day off. Don't fake your manager's signature. Don't pretend that a client is at your dinner so you can write it off as a business expense. You can easily be caught. At worst, you might be fired.

- Don't take or make personal calls at work until you are established in your job. Always keep personal calls to a minimum. People can overhear what you are saying. If you must make a personal call, try to make it from your cell phone or use an empty office or conference room.

- Don't steal anything from the workplace. An occasional Kleenex box or post-it note is understandable, but not office artwork, telephones or computers. That's larceny. Many companies have hidden video cameras in the office supply room.

- Don't use your work e-mail for personal business. Your company's Information Technology (IT) department (or worse yet, your boss) can view your work e-mail account. And don't think you can maintain your privacy just by deleting personal messages – everything is recoverable from the company server and backup tapes. Remember that you have no recourse or protection of privacy when you are using your employer's equipment. In addition, if you segregate your work and personal e-mail accounts, you will work more efficiently and be less distracted. Use an online e-mail service like Yahoo! or Hotmail for personal communications.

- Don't pad your hours. If you are in a client services company, make sure you understand your company's policy on billing. For example, find out at what increments your company bills out your time (e.g., in blocks of six minutes, ten minutes, one hour, etc.) and how you should bill if you go over that increment. Accurate billing helps generate better estimates for future projects for clients, so don't cut your hours either. Also, find out the company policy on vacations. Some places don't count days out of the office as vacation days when you check your voice mail regularly and are available by phone. Others do.

Office Parties

Most companies will host the occasional department-wide or company-wide happy hour or holiday party, and sometimes even bridal showers, baby showers and birthday parties for specific employees. Do not be fooled – just because it is called a "party" doesn't mean you can cut loose like you do with friends. Losing control at an office party is an easy way to lose the respect of your co-workers and superiors.

Observe the normal guidelines of professional behavior and party manners to have the best time:

- Find out the exact hours of the event. Figure out whether it is an open house where you can come and go as you please or a formal gathering where guests are expected there for the duration. A consulting analyst showed up at a "barbecue" hosted at a partner's house a couple of hours after the designated start time expecting a casual event, only to find that everyone had already eaten a catered sit-down meal.

- Do not dress provocatively or extremely casually. (Leave the midriff-baring tops and the stained sweatshirts at home.) Wearing a more colorful outfit or fun accessories to celebrate the occasion is OK.

- Stay sober.

IMPORTANT: Some companies or departments encourage a sort of machismo when it comes to partying. Sales departments and investment banks are known for this practice. All employees are expected to "party hard" in order to be considered part of the team. Your manager may even egg you on to drink too much. Don't succumb to this pressure. Even if you become intoxicated and embarrass yourself due to your manager's influence, it is your own professional credibility that will be called into question – perhaps even by your own manager! At the same time, it is important to reap the benefits of the bonding and networking that happens out of the office. Fortunately, there are tricks to look like you are indulging much more than you are.

- Drink slowly. Nurse a drink the whole night, so you always have something in your hand.

- Eat plenty of carbohydrates, which will dilute the effect of the alcohol. Often, happy hours or parties happen at the end of the work day before you have a chance to eat dinner. Keep some snacks in the office or grab food on the way to the party. Eat the chips and pretzels at the party.

- Alternate alcoholic and non-alcoholic drinks that look alike, e.g., gin and tonic and club soda, or screwdrivers and pure orange juice.

Visit Vault at **www.vault.com** for insider company profiles, expert advice, career message boards, expert resume reviews, the Vault Job Board and more.

VAULT CAREER LIBRARY   29

People will think you are drinking more than you are. If you like, you can stick to the non-alcoholic alternatives.

- If the drinks are free, exchange unfinished drinks for fresh drinks. Changing drinks often makes it look like you are drinking more than you are.

- Even if you're not drinking, you can still be merry. Joke around and be friendly – your drunker co-workers probably won't even notice the difference.

- Watch your table manners, even if you're not literally sitting at a table. There is nothing worse than stuffing your face with more than your fair share of food and then chewing with your mouth open. If you plan on meeting senior executives, swallow your food and check your teeth first. If you eat like an animal, your manager may be wary of sending you to business dinners. You might consider eating before the event.

- Do not hit on people you find attractive.

- Do not complain about your job, even in a joking manner.

- Do not touch anyone excessively. What you think is affectionate, others may find creepy.

- Do not share any personal information with co-workers that will diminish your professional credibility.

- Don't bring a date or other guest without checking first to make sure it's all right to do so.

Have a Few Good Business Dates in Your Rolodex

Eric Keene, former McKinsey consultant

If your company is very family- or couples-oriented but you are single, you may want to consider bringing a good friend to your work functions, even if he or she is not a romantic partner of yours. Another set of eyes and ears never hurts. But make sure your date is low maintenance and corporate enough to fit into the event; otherwise, you will have to babysit your date and would probably be better off going alone.

Office Politics

The term "office politics" has an extremely negative connotation. It suggests backstabbing, vicious maneuvering and general negativity. But office politics is actually a neutral term. You will inevitably "play" office politics if you work in a company. Simply following the written and unwritten rules of Corporate America means that you are involved in office politics. Coming in at the right time, being especially nice to certain people, doing your work in a certain way – it all falls under the rubric of office politics.

The biggest mistake people make is to think that one either participates in office politics in a nasty way, or not at all. So often people will say, "I have no interest in playing THAT game." You cannot avoid office politics. What you can do is participate in an ethical manner.

The term "office politics" is often applied to the sometimes nasty conflicts that arise in a company when two or more factions in the office compete to get support for their own agenda. The factions could be individual people, teams, departments or divisions. Any issue can become the fodder for a political conflict. Let's say two companies merge. The senior executives of each company will try to keep their jobs and get their counterparts demoted or downsized. Sometimes different departments try to curry the favor of the CEO in order to win a bigger chunk of the budget for their own projects. Sometimes junior managers will badmouth or even sabotage each other's work, jockeying for the limited number of senior management positions.

Generally speaking, entry-level employees have little to no control over nasty office politics. But you can exert some control on how much you will be affected if you are caught in the middle of a heated political battle. Just because your department head is locking horns with another department head doesn't mean you can't build friendly relationships with individuals on both sides of a struggle. Aligning yourself with one side of a struggle when you have nothing to gain from the outcome is a potential career-limiting move. The best thing to do as a new hire is to stay out of political struggles around the office as much as possible. Don't verbalize support for any one side if the situation does not involve you or impact your life. Let superiors sort the conflicts out. Hone your skills in terms of following the rules of your office and thriving in the system. That's the kind of politics you can win at and feel good about.

Visit Vault at **www.vault.com** for insider company profiles, expert advice, career message boards, expert resume reviews, the Vault Job Board and more.

V\ULT CAREER LIBRARY   **31**

Categorizing the Corporate World

CHAPTER 3

Company Structure

Corporate America comes in many forms, but most companies are structured as either a partnership or corporation. How your company is organized directly affects its power structure.

In a general partnership, a group of partners shares the right to manage the company and participate in the profits. That means the partners hold all the power. Partners are responsible for selling work to clients. The more work a partner generates and bills to clients (in business lingo, the bigger a "rainmaker" he is), the more money the firm and that partner make at the end of the year, and therefore the more influence that partner has on the firm's management.

In a corporation, executive officers manage the company and shareholders invest in the company, though they are not liable for the company's activities. The executive team is supervised by the board of directors, a committee of accomplished business people, to represent shareholder interests. The board generally meets four times a year to review and direct major management decisions. Many corporations' shares are publicly traded on a stock exchange, opening their finances to public scrutiny. Corporations are also subject to pressure by investors to keep profits high.

Big Company vs. Small Company

There is no "better" or "worse" in working for a huge corporation versus working for a somewhat smaller concern. Some companies may be better for you, however.

Experience

At a larger company, you may have more opportunity to work with different teams and different departments. Depending on the structure of the teams, you may become more of a specialist within your profession if you end up focusing on one small piece of each project. Your professional growth and promotional opportunities may be subject to an inflexible bureaucratic process and tenure timeline. At the same time, there will be alternative career

Visit Vault at **www.vault.com** for insider company profiles, expert advice, career message boards, expert resume reviews, the Vault Job Board and more.

VAULT CAREER LIBRARY   33

paths, either in your own department or in other departments. Your employer will also probably enjoy greater name recognition, always an asset when you are applying for jobs outside the company.

At a smaller company, or in a small department, you may be more of a generalist, or "jack-of-all-trades," because it is harder for a small team to get everything done if everyone sticks to rigid job descriptions. You may find yourself pulled onto different projects that need an extra hand as deadlines grow near. You will enjoy earlier exposure to higher-level responsibilities, such as interacting with senior staff and external clients. On the other end of the spectrum, you may have heavier administrative burdens, like word processing, copying and distributing data, and mailing or delivering packages.

Small companies can be more flexible in terms of giving you the title, responsibilities and compensation that you deserve as soon as you earn them – they have more to lose if they lose a good performer. You are likely to achieve a higher level of responsibility sooner than you would at a big company. Your company may also occupy a business niche that particularly interests you, and may help you become an expert in a certain field at a younger age.

Pick a Company where You Can Stand out
Software developer

At the end of my senior year in college, I had several job offers, both from large and small companies. Ultimately, I accepted a position in a small group within a medium-sized company. I was the twelfth employee in the group, and it had only hired two or three people that year. I ended up going with that company largely because I liked the people who had interviewed me and was excited about the work I'd be doing.

In retrospect, it was a great personal career choice for another reason – the group was a place where I could stand out and be noticed. First, my computer science background happened to be a perfect fit for the position (which was not the case with other offers, where my computer science skills would hardly be used), and second, the small group size helped others recognize my solid contributions.

Resources

Generally speaking, the bigger the company, the more expansive the resources. Advantages can include more formal training programs, mentoring programs, large client databases, an organized library of reference materials, and staffing support from researchers, assistants, word processors and file clerks, who allow you to focus on more substantial work. For your personal growth, a big company may also provide attractive benefits like free or subsidized meals, tuition reimbursement and a gym membership.

Small companies offer a personalized touch. You may get more direct training from, and better access to, your managers. Because there are fewer staff resources to share the work, you may develop a skillset both broader and deeper than that of working at a large company. Without a library of research at your fingertips, you will hone your research skills digging for and organizing data from all sources of information, internal and external, online and offline.

Be Flexible about Location for the Best Professional Opportunity
Eric Keene, former McKinsey consultant

I tell new graduates to let the company be the most important selection factor when coming out of school, not location. You can work anywhere for two to three years. Too many folks limit their job opportunities geographically way too early in their career.

Culture

A big company is typically more bureaucratic and slower to change than small companies. Because a large company is so rule-bound, you may need special dispensation to do something different from your colleagues. For example, according to a former auditor at an international accounting firm, an employee who preferred not to travel needed to have a special note put in the staffing file in order for the company to "accommodate" those needs. Be forewarned that different departments may have different cultures, sometimes even antagonistic rivalries, and your experience will largely depend on which department you are in. While varying cultures may exist at once, a large company may put more deliberate effort into developing a positive corporate culture, training management to be accessible role models and providing lots of fun activities for team-building. Larger companies are also more likely to

Visit Vault at **www.vault.com** for insider company profiles, expert advice, career message boards, expert resume reviews, the Vault Job Board and more.

VAULT CAREER LIBRARY   35

have established clubs and networking organizations for women and minorities.

A small company usually has a more coherent culture, which is great if you fit in and problematic if you don't. If you dislike someone, you will be hard-pressed to avoid him or her. The advantage of a small company may be the speed of decision-making and your ability to impact cultural change. There will probably be fewer fringe benefits, and even your basic health care plan may not be as good. If you are outgoing and enjoy planning activities for your friends, you may enjoy playing the informal role of social guru or training coordinator in the office.

Socially

At a large company, you will start with a larger class of new hires who are all eager to make friends (like freshman year in college). You will also have many more colleagues with various backgrounds and personalities. On the other hand, the larger the company, the more insular each department can become. You may need to take the initiative to meet your colleagues outside of your department.

At a small company, you will get to know everyone better, not just the people who share your function or are in your hiring class. There is less social division along department lines because the departments are each so small. And while no environment is completely free of politics, you have a higher chance of finding a tight-knit community in a smaller company.

Shine in a Small Company

Jimmy Si, former IBM employee, current senior account executive, Gartner Group

I think it is harder to move up in a big company. Big companies retain their employees by offering good salaries, stable jobs and great benefits. People get comfortable in their positions. But if you really want to have a lot of responsibility and make a lot of money, you have to get into a small company where you can really stand out. It's good to mix things up and have experiences in both big and small companies, so you don't become complacent in a comfortable but boring job.

Client Services vs. In-House

There are two broad types of industries: client services and in-house. The client service industry provides professional services, including accounting, advertising, banking, consulting and legal, to other companies. The focus of the client service industry is getting and keeping clients to generate revenue for the company. Working in-house means you are part of a company that makes a product (e.g., manufacturing, entertainment, consumer products, software, etc.). Your company's goals are to maximize sales of its products while minimizing the costs of making and selling that product to generate the greatest profit.

Your job focus and responsibilities will differ according to whether you are in a client service company or in-house. If you are in the client services industry, you are likely starting on the lowest rung of the partner track. Depending on your company, you will either be assigned to a set team under one partner or to rotating teams. You will be supporting your manager on client work on a daily basis, and interacting with the client under your manager's guidance. In this environment, time equals money. The client is billed for your team's time, either by the hour or at a negotiated flat fee based on a projection of total hours needed to deliver a project. The more skilled you become, the higher your billing rate. The longer you take to execute a task in the flat fee scenario, the more money your employer loses on you. The number of hours you bill and your contributions to keeping the client happy are of the utmost importance. Repeat client business is always a much easier way to make money than constantly drumming up new clients.

If you are in-house at a company, you are probably part of an internal department with a particular function contributing to either operations or administration. Operations manages the development, production or sale of your company's products as part of a department. Examples: product development, business development, marketing, engineering, sales. Administration manages the people, systems or resources of the company. Examples: human resources, legal, information technology, accounting.

On a daily basis, you will be directly supporting managers and directors specializing in your same function, and collaborating with other functional departments to maximize your company's sales and minimize overhead costs. It depends on your company whether you will have specific or diverse responsibilities for one or many products. The customers for your products will be other businesses or individual people.

Visit Vault at **www.vault.com** for insider company profiles, expert advice, career message boards, expert resume reviews, the Vault Job Board and more.

VAULT CAREER LIBRARY   **37**

The distinction isn't always clear-cut – you may be, for example, a sales assistant (and therefore in client services) in a company that produces software, or in an HR function (providing in-house support) in a client service company.

Be Where the Action Is
Jimmy Si, senior account executive, Gartner Group

Look for a job that is on the "front line" of action in your company if you want a dynamic career opportunity. Whatever your company does, be where the action is. For example, if your company manufactures a product, the best jobs would be developing the product or selling the product to clients. Don't be in the back office working on internal administration projects. If you are not part of teams directly generating revenues for the company, you will have less opportunity to move up.

ON THE JOB

Organization and Time Management Skills

CHAPTER 4

Organization and time management skills are crucial in any corporate job. Here's how to situate yourself when you start your job and ensure you manage your time and your work well.

Orienting Yourself

Your first day

On your first day, your role is simply to ensure that you show up on time and fill out paperwork. Find out when to arrive and where to go. Budget plenty of wiggle room to ensure that you're on time. Bring two forms of identification with you for employment purposes; your passport or driver's license and social security card work best. You may also have to designate an emergency contact and a life insurance recipient. Read your orientation materials carefully.

Introduce yourself to your new colleagues right away. The best-case scenario is that people will come up to you to greet you on your first day, but this doesn't always happen. Don't be shy; walk around and introduce yourself. It is perfectly appropriate to knock on the door of your neighbor or approach nearby cubicles and say, "Hi, I'm Carla. I started today in Joe Smith's group. I'm working down the hall from you, so I'm sure I'll be seeing you often." Or ask your human resources coordinator or your new boss to take you on a tour and introduce people. The golden opportunity to meet everyone is during your first couple of months on the job. The longer you wait, the more awkward it becomes to introduce yourself to someone you have been passing in the halls or riding elevators with for months now.

Find your resources. Ask for a tour of the online and offline office resources: equipment, reference materials, stock room and anything else that you need.

Meet company experts. In your first few weeks, introduce yourself to key players, from your boss' boss to the office manager. Make sure you identify yourself by department and manager so these busy people will be able to place you. For example, you could say, "Hi Kathy, I'm Carla, and I just joined Joe Smith's group. I started as an analyst here this week, and heard

Visit Vault at **www.vault.com** for insider company profiles, expert advice, career message boards, expert resume reviews, the Vault Job Board and more.

VAULT CAREER LIBRARY 41

your name mentioned in the Project X meeting." You should also introduce yourself to all the assistants in your office; assistants often control access to key people or information.

Join clubs. If you are interested in mentoring organizations, such as an association of Asian employees, try to make contact via e-mail in your first month or so on the job.

Tracing the Pathways of Power

Along with the firm's physical layout, you must learn your firm's power layout. Be patient but deliberate in gathering this information, which is essential to navigating and succeeding in any corporate environment. You should know:

- **The organization chart.** Start with the basics. What are the various divisions and departments in your company? Who heads each one? Organization (normally called "org") charts are often available on your company's intranet.

Tutorial on titles: The pecking order

	Client-Service Company	In-house Company
Top	Partner	Executive Vice President*
	Engagement Manager	Senior Vice President*
	Manager	Vice President
	Senior Associate	Director
	Associate	Manager
Entry Level	Analyst, Associate, Consultant	Assistant, Staff, Coordinator

May also be corporate officers, such as CEO, COO, Treasurer, Secretary, etc.

- **Where the power base resides.** Does the sales or finance department call the shots? Who within each of these departments holds the real power? What are the politics between the senior executives? Does your boss have any power? Will there be a power shift soon?

Recognize the Power Base
Product manager at a dot-com

At my company, the power shifted almost quarterly. Power can be both good and bad. When the company first started in late 1999, the founder and CEO had all the power due to his reputation and bank account from his other company, a billion-dollar powerhouse. Whatever he said went.

By early 2000, the power shifted to the sales force with the hiring of a new VP of sales. Anything sales wanted was a "silver bullet," and the entire company worked on those projects. If your project wasn't one of the silver bullets, you could forget about getting resources or support. However, in late 2000, the power moved to engineering in a negative way, because the VP of engineering could not deliver the platform as promised. Thus, all resources got focused on getting the platform out the door. All other work became secondary.

In 2001, my company hired a new VP of marketing, and suddenly he was our new savior. During that year, different projects held sway over the company. If you were not working on these projects, you had a very difficult time getting executive attention. By the end of the year, that VP had lost his luster and the company was searching for a new VP. Those who had clung to his shooting star found themselves fading as well.

Try to work for the department where the power resides, but pay attention to the power within the group since it may shift subtly but quickly. You may find that a project that had everyone's support and attention last quarter is suddenly ignored. Thus, try to build as much success and momentum when you do have power. When you're out of the limelight, lower your expectations, build support, and make sure your i's are dotted and t's are crossed. Finally, watch out for betting your reputation on following one star too closely. You'll enjoy the ride up, but the flameout can be brutal. Try to be a team player throughout. You never know when the power tides will shift.

Establish and Maintain an Organizational System

Now that you know how your company works, you need to make sure you're organized as well. If there's one thing you can do to help yourself succeed in a corporate environment, it's developing superb organizational skills. You will be judged on your personal organization and the appearance of your office, files or cube. You also will be judged on the speed with which you can find a document, a phone number or your notes. When your manager asks you for version six of the document that's now on version 13, either you will have that file accurately named, dated, and saved in the right folder on your computer, or you will get down on your hands and knees and start sorting through your recycling box.

While you'll naturally become more efficient as you gain experience and start seeing the same types of work over and over again, you can get a head start by developing smart, meticulous work habits and using the tools and resources at your disposal. Here are some things that will help you organize your work life.

- **Find out where the company's shared main files are kept** and what you have to put in them. For example, law firms often require files be kept by client and by chronology. Make sure you are (or your assistant is) filing accordingly and in a timely manner.

- **Follow the department filing system for hard and electronic documents**, so that you can find key documents quickly. If there is no corporate naming standard, an alphabetical system is easiest. Name each matter something obvious (e.g., by client name and the date) and clearly indicate all versions up to the most current. For example, an analysis of IBM's return on investment done on September 15, 2003, could be called "IBM_ROI_Analysis_091503.xls."

- **Have someone to back you up.** Show at least one person in the office how you have organized your files so they can find things in your absence.

- **Have an inbox** so people know where to drop things off for you. Otherwise, they will just drop documents on your desk, where they may be misplaced. Go through your inbox daily so it doesn't pile up. Everything in your inbox should be either immediately discarded, filed or put in your to-do pile. If you must leave a file for someone who does not have an inbox, leave it facedown on his chair.

- **Organize your to-do pile.** Assign deadlines and calendar items in your to-do pile so nothing falls through the cracks. Create notes to remind yourself when a deadline is approaching (e.g., one month away, two weeks away, two days away). A written list of items that you cross off is low-tech, but very helpful.

- **Throw out clutter.** Do not leave things in your inbox more than one day, or in your to-do pile past the deadline assigned.

- **Create a list of key phone numbers** (external clients and internal extensions), to keep with you at all times. If you have to unexpectedly return a phone call after hours or on the weekend, you will be glad you don't have to drive into the office to find the number.

- **Get on standard and special distribution lists** to keep updated on changes to important phone numbers, policies, meeting schedules, etc. You can ask admins or junior people on the team for these lists. Keep this information on your Palm Pilot (if you have one) and cell phone.

- **Keep one master calendar.** Consult it daily and weekly to make sure you are on top of approaching deadlines and meetings. Bring it to meetings so you can check key dates or note the dates of future meetings. If your calendar is electronic, set reminders to sound an alarm before each meeting to keep you on time.

- **Do your best not to work late.** Tasks grow to fill the time allotted, so don't let a task spill over past quitting time or into the weekend. A common procrastination technique is not to do any real work during the day and then "catch up" after 5 p.m. or on weekends. This method is OK on occasion if you find it difficult to get work done during the day (due to meetings, telephone calls and other distractions), but it can be a bad habit to get into. In general, you will find that you are not more productive – your per hour productivity will most likely decrease, as well as the quality of your work, because you will be tired and more likely to burn out. And waiting until after everyone has gone home to get work done can mean that other people will not be around to give you crucial feedback and information.

- **Don't forget to alternate work with breaks.** Nothing will hold your attention 100 percent of the time, and staring at your computer screen doesn't count as work. Break your work into thirty-minute chunks, alternating with smaller tasks or something fun, like personal e-mail or Instant Messenger (IM).

Visit Vault at **www.vault.com** for insider company profiles, expert advice, career message boards, expert resume reviews, the Vault Job Board and more.

VAULT CAREER LIBRARY   **45**

> ## PDA Bliss
> ### Former Parthenon consultant
>
> As far as organization goes, there is no better invention than the Palm Pilot and its syncing capacity with Microsoft Outlook. I'll admit to a slow adoption rate, but once I received a Palm as a birthday gift (and forced myself to use it), my life gained tremendous organizational clarity. Moreover, I no longer forget birthdays and anniversaries. I even get a reminder to send a card!

- **Keep all your daily notes in one notebook.** Keep to-do lists, notes from phone conversations and other records in one notebook. You'll be able to find information much more easily.

- **Perfectionism is a trap.** Not every thing you do must be perfect. High quality performance also means smart use of resources. If you find yourself spending hours laboring over an e-mail to a co-worker or endlessly revising the layout of a draft document, you may be spending far too much energy on inconsequential details. While over-delivering is heroic, you don't want to squander your time and resources. So if you have promised an outline, deliver an outline, not the final product.

Multitasking

Getting pulled in a million directions is the biggest enemy of efficiency. When you juggle multiple projects, managers and clients, you will find yourself switching gears many times during the day, depending on who is on the phone and what deadline is approaching first. The more times you switch gears, the more productive time you will lose during the day. Identify what is most important. When you must work hard on one project, minimize the number of transitions during your day, as much as possible.

- **Set aside blocks of time to focus on a single important project.** If you are juggling multiple projects, rank them by importance and focus a set amount of time on the most important project. You may need to come in over the weekend to get a block of uninterrupted time. One exception: if you get a request that will take less than five minutes to complete (and you won't jeopardize more important projects), just finish it immediately, especially if it comes from your manager.

- **Remove distractions.** Turn off your ringer and start ignoring your e-mail. Turn off your instant messenger. Block time on your electronic calendar, especially if the rest of the company can see your schedule online. Give yourself a designated time to respond to calls and e-mails, instead of accepting every call and replying to every e-mail the moment you get it.

Don't Waste Time on E-mail
Jimmy Si, senior account executive, Gartner Group

Replying to e-mail can become a huge waste of time. People sit at their desks crafting perfect responses to every e-mail they receive. Some people write e-mails that are pages long. Not every e-mail in your inbox warrants a reply especially if it does not directly contribute to the bottom line. Spend your time at work doing things that directly contribute to one objective or another. Replying to e-mails all day long accomplishes nothing.

Prioritize! Observe the 80/20 Rule

The Pareto Principle was derived by a 19th century Italian economist who observed that 20 percent of the people (later termed the "vital few" as opposed to the remaining 80 percent, or the "trivial many") controlled 80 percent of the land, money and influence in Italy. This ratio has been applied broadly to business and time management concepts. On a corporate level, generally 20 percent of a company's clients or products generate 80 percent of company sales. On a personal level, 20 percent of your effort will generate 80 percent of your results, and 20 percent of your results will consume 80 percent of your time, resources, and efforts.

Figure out how the 80/20 rule applies to your own time management practices. You must be disciplined in identifying and prioritizing the most important 20 percent of your work. Distinguish between "urgent" and "important" tasks. Many urgent tasks are not important.

Efficiency comes with the appropriate prioritization of your work, and either delegating or ignoring low priority but time-consuming "urgent" tasks. A common time-wasting trap is to knock out easy but low priority tasks first in order to put off working on an important but difficult assignment.

Visit Vault at **www.vault.com** for insider company profiles, expert advice, career message boards, expert resume reviews, the Vault Job Board and more.

V/\ULT CAREER LIBRARY   **47**

First Things First
Former brand management analyst

Do what's asked for first! I was working on a project once where I showed a draft of a project to my manager a few days before presenting it in a meeting. She wrote out several comments for me that I figured were minor changes that I could finish in 10 minutes.

So for the next day, I thought I would spend time creating another part of the presentation that I thought would be much more impressive and would "wow" her. In any case, I forgot about her changes because they were so minor.

When I presented the presentation to her again, not only did she not care about my additional work, but her only questions were about the notes she gave me in the prior meeting. I learned too late that I should have reprioritized my work.

Be Reliable

It will not matter if you are well-organized if you're not delivering results. Do what you say you will do. If you keep overpromising, others will stop trusting your ability to deliver. It's probably better to underpromise and overdeliver.

For people to rely on you, you need to:

• **Meet deadlines.** If you tell a partner, peer or client that you are going to do something, deliver on time. Your work affects other timelines. For example, you may be asked to research the market share for a certain product by a certain time because that information will be used in a larger analysis that is due the next day.

If you can't meet a deadline, let any parties affected know as early as possible and specify a revised estimated delivery time.

• **Pin down the deadline as specifically as possible.** For example, if a partner assigns a project to be delivered Wednesday, find out if he means Wednesday morning or Wednesday afternoon, or if Thursday morning is actually OK.

- **Follow through on requests, regardless of priority.** It makes you look bad if someone has to ask you more than once for an assignment. Your to-do list will come in especially handy here.

- **Anticipate details.** There are a lot of little tasks that need to be done during the day that no one will remind you to do, like filing your latest documents in your own files and on a shared drive for the office, documenting your hours on timesheets and turning in your expense reports. You won't always get credit for being on top of daily maintenance, but your managers and clients will notice when you drop the ball.

Visit Vault at **www.vault.com** for insider company profiles, expert advice, career message boards, expert resume reviews, the Vault Job Board and more.

VAULT CAREER LIBRARY   49

Communication Skills

No matter the company or industry, you will need to communicate effectively with your clients, boss and peers via the phone, computer and in person. Choose your communication technique wisely.

Be Clear, Concise and Thorough

Business communications need to be as short and direct as possible. At the same time, you must thoroughly explain yourself. Never assume that your audience has the same knowledge you do.

Open with the topic at hand. Make sure that your audience knows from the opening of your communication what topic you are addressing.

- In an e-mail, use the subject line and first sentence to state the subject. Guessing at the contents of an e-mail is annoying, especially when you are looking through your e-mail archives for an important past communication. Find out if people with BlackBerries (or other personal digital assistants with e-mail options) like to have the question posed to them in the subject line of the e-mail.

- In a document, the title and opening sentence should state the main topic.

- Keep all voice mails under two minutes whenever possible. Meandering voice mails are annoying and inefficient. Tell the person what you want to discuss in the voice mail, and then follow up by e-mail or in person.

- If you must leave a detailed voice mail message, say in the beginning of the voice mail how many points you have, and then enumerate each point. If you are leaving a message for multiple people, identify all the participants. For example, you could say, "This is Joan leaving a message for John and Mary regarding client X. X wants three things. One, X wants the product launch timeline via e-mail today. Two, X wants the weekly meeting scheduled for Monday changed to Tuesday. Three, X wants the engagement manager to fly out right after this meeting."

Visit Vault at **www.vault.com** for insider company profiles, expert advice, career message boards, expert resume reviews, the Vault Job Board and more.

VAULT CAREER LIBRARY 51

> **IMPORTANT:** Never, ever send personal e-mails about questionable activities undertaken on company time. One young Korean-American man working at an international company bragged to a few of his friends of his sexual and material exploits in Seoul. His explicit, immature e-mail was forwarded around the world and made its way to several international newspapers. Needless to say, he was fired.

Lead with facts and findings in your communication and follow with your own opinions and recommendations. If you're at a meeting, start with an agenda and end with group discussion and debate. Too often, the presentation of your work is confused or derailed by a debate sparked by a single issue that takes over the entire conversation. Make sure people understand that your presentation will address several issues further on, and major debates should be reserved until the end. When presenting in person, you may want to pass out an agenda or write the bullet points on the board to keep people on track (and to signal to them what you are talking about).

Organize your thoughts in sections or bullet points. Your audience should be able to scan your document, e-mail, or their notes from your verbal conversation, and immediately identify the highlights. Make it easier for them by actually bullet-pointing or numbering your main points. If you are writing in sections or paragraphs, your reader should be able to read the first sentence of each paragraph and understand your message.

Address your audience in e-mails: If you have different questions for different readers, draw their attention to the section of your e-mail relating to them by putting their names in bold and caps there. You'll have a better chance that they will address your concerns. If you have a lot of action items associated with many different people, it may be more effective just to send separate e-mails so you don't lose anyone.

Purge redundancies in your points. Make sure each individual point conveys a new thought. Combine similar points into one.

Avoid overuse of subjective adjectives and adverbs. Don't muddy the facts and findings with too many subjective phrases that may sway your audience's opinion before they understand the full context of the work. For example, "unfortunately," "surprisingly," "disappointingly," reveal subjective opinions that should be reserved for discussion.

Purge conversational filler. Train yourself to avoid unprofessional and distracting conversational filler words, such as "you know," "like," "so" and "anyway" in your business communication. Post a list of words to avoid by your phone to keep them in mind during business calls. When you leave a voice mail for someone, listen to it again before sending it to gauge your coherence and brevity. Make sure you know the system lets you erase and re-record before you decide to try again.

Be comfortable with silent pauses in an oral presentation or in a group discussion as your audience reads a slide or digests what you have said before moving on to your next point. Don't try to fill every moment with talk. Don't panic because you paused to remember a point or if you got sidetracked; these pauses are always shorter than they feel.

Outline what you want to say in a meeting or on a phone call. It's tough to get a group together on a call or in a meeting. Addressing all of your critical points in one conversation is particularly important. If you do forget something, follow up immediately by phone or e-mail.

The Ten Commandments of E-mail
(Paraphrased from an article in *PC World*, original author unknown)

1) Include a clear and specific subject line.

2) Edit text down to the minimum needed.

3) Read your message three times before sending it.

4) Consider how the recipient might react to your message.

5) Check your spelling and grammar.

6) Do not curse, flame, spam or use all caps.

7) Never forward a chain letter.

8) Do not use e-mail for any illegal or unethical purpose.

9) Do not rely on the privacy of e-mail.

10) When in doubt, save your message overnight and reread it the next day.

IMPORTANT: Don't send an e-mail or a voice mail when you are mad! Let yourself cool down before you react. You don't want a permanent record of your emotional response towards a colleague or a client. What you say in the heat of the moment can get you into a lot of trouble later.

Visit Vault at www.vault.com for insider company profiles, expert advice, career message boards, expert resume reviews, the Vault Job Board and more.

V/\ULT CAREER LIBRARY   53

Tailor Your Communication Approach to Your Audience

It doesn't matter how brilliant your work and ideas are if you don't do a good job presenting them. Consider your audience's personality and level of knowledge on the topic when preparing your content. For example, if it's a meeting with your peers, you probably can be more relaxed and casual. If you are bringing together a diverse group, you may need to walk briefly through the history of the issue or explain the meaning of some words before you launch into a discussion.

Anticipate your listeners' concerns and preemptively address them. Some people want a lot of detail up front to understand fully the context of the topic before considering your analyses and recommendations; others want you to summarize the issue briefly, deliver the bottom line findings up front and then let them delve into the detail on their own time. Some people are very numbers-oriented and easily navigate charts and graphs; others are more comfortable with qualitative concepts and need to be slowly walked through charts, graphs and even simple analyses.

The unproductive debates that consume some meetings are often fueled by conflicting communication styles rather than disagreements over fundamental issues of content. The more you understand how to adapt your communication style to your audience and facilitate discussion between individuals with different communication styles, the more time you can focus on discussing substantial issues. Here are some tips to help you prepare for your presentations.

• Read up on some basic professional personality assessment tools in order to spot people's styles, understand how they differ from yours, and work together most effectively. Myers-Briggs is probably the best known of these tools. These personality assessment tools help you distinguish between different styles of processing information and expressing opinions. You can evaluate your own personality online at http://www.humanmetrics.com/cgi-win/JTypes2.asp.

• Hand out an agenda before the meeting or write one down on a whiteboard to help keep the group focused.

• If you are presenting to a group of people, try to have enough detail to accommodate the most minutiae-focused participant, but put it in an appendix or a separate hand-out for those inclined to review on their own time. Make it clear that you have as much detail as people need, but want to review the big picture with the group first rather than slowing down the body of the presentation with all the specifics. Be prepared to move people along if the meeting bogs down, and you don't think you can hit all the points in the allotted time (e.g., say, "That's a good point – I'd like to follow up with you on that after this meeting.")

- Proactively offer to set up one-on-one offline meetings with people to walk them through the detail. People may be embarrassed to ask for more explanation even if they don't understand something.

- Observe and emulate the style of the most articulate, persuasive speakers in your office.

IMPORTANT: Challenge others in a nonthreatening, impersonal way.

Respect the opinions of others, as you would want others to respect yours.

- Never use words that reflect intelligence in challenging someone else's opinion, such as "stupid," "illogical," "absurd," and "nonsensical." Always use euphemisms to present your idea, such as "alternative," "appropriate," "more reflective," etc.

- Don't make a point of attributing the wrong opinion to someone else (e.g., "Your opinion"), and the right opinion to yourself (e.g., "My opinion").

- Substitute "and" for "but." People identify "but" and "however" as words that preface a contradiction to their opinion, which makes people tune out what you're about to say.

- Preface an opposing remark you are about to make with "I understand your point," "I hear you," or "That's a great point."

For example:

"Your analysis made these assumptions, but I think my assumptions are more logical."

versus

"The last draft of the analysis made certain assumptions, and I think we have new assumptions more reflective of the current market situation."

Visit Vault at **www.vault.com** for insider company profiles, expert advice, career message boards, expert resume reviews, the Vault Job Board and more.

VAULT CAREER LIBRARY

55

Day-To-Day Skills

CHAPTER 6

Every day you will be performing routine tasks, making phone calls, organizing or attending meetings and analyzing data. This chapter discusses the most efficient ways to execute these tasks.

Phone Skills

Good phone habits:

- Keep your notebook and pen by your phone at all times. In a pinch, open up an e-mail, take notes as you speak, then e-mail your notes to yourself.

- When you call someone for an involved discussion, do not jump into your questions if the call is not scheduled – ask if it is a convenient time to talk. If it is not, reschedule.

- Do not put anyone on hold for more than one minute (especially if your company has annoying hold music). Get back on the line and say you will call back once you have found the person or the information you need.

- Don't talk to people on speaker phone unless you have a good reason – for example, if there are multiple people on your end or you need to look through files or type while you are talking. Let the person know you are putting her on speaker phone for a specific reason. Otherwise it comes across as arrogant. Also, turn down the volume so you don't bother your neighbors.

- If a client or manager calls with questions for you, write the questions down and call back with all of the answers. Don't keep them on the phone while you scramble for the information.

- Return business-related phone calls by the end of each work day. Colleagues and clients will judge your responsiveness by how quickly you return phone calls. You may want to follow up a voice mail message with an e-mail. That way you'll have a written record.

- Learn the phone system, especially how to put people on hold and not hang up on them. Also, make sure you know how to teleconference and transfer callers. You may want to practice on co-workers first. There usually is a handbook for your phone with a cheat sheet of the most important functions.

Know the Phone System
Product manager

During the interview process for the job that I ultimately accepted after college, I had to call the head of the company to schedule a phone interview. When I called, I received his voice mail and decided to leave a message. When I finished leaving what was a perfectly acceptable voice mail, I pressed 1 for more options instead of simply hanging up. I was drawn to option 3 to "erase and re-record", because I hadn't left the perfectly articulated message. Fifteen minutes and six or seven attempts later (where I thought I had mastered the art of pressing 1 and then 3), I hadn't left anything better than the first message, and I was getting increasingly frustrated. Midway through the next attempt, I fumbled on some words, stopped mid-sentence, said "shit, that sucked", and then pressed 1. But, instead of pressing 3 to "erase and re-record", I accidentally pressed 1 to "deliver this message". I must have pressed every key on the phone to return to the prompt for "erase and re-record", but no such luck. Embarrassed, I called right back and left a succinct apology and request to schedule the phone interview – on my first attempt. I landed the job, but not without some egg on my face! So, either be careful with the voice mail options, or be happy with your first message and then just hang up.

- When you hang up the phone, make sure you have hung up the phone! If you want to continue a conversation with one person at the end of a conference call, tell that person you will call him back. Don't just stay on the line and ask everyone else to hang up.

- Be careful with the "mute" button. You may think the other side can't hear what you're saying, but sometimes the mute button doesn't work or you don't press it correctly.

Unintended Recording
Former management consultant

A friend of mine at a competing strategy consulting company in San Francisco left a casual voice mail for me one afternoon on speaker phone, but did not properly end the call after he was done leaving the message. The next ten minutes of his conversation were entirely enlightening, both on a professional and social level! Fortunately, he's one of my best friends and his message was immediately deleted (well, after I listened to it twice). But there could have been potentially devastating results had he done this with someone else.

Hunting someone down by phone:

- If you need to find someone urgently and get voice mail, press "0" for the operator and have the person paged.

- You can also press "0" and ask the assistant/operator to hunt the person down, or ask for the person's cell phone number. Assistants are quite responsive to clients. Explaining the emergency may lead to a quicker response.

- Alternatively, redial the person's phone number with a one-digit difference. You may reach her neighbor, whom you can ask to track the person down for you.

- Leave one voice mail, and try to call periodically (e.g., every hour) without leaving a message – if it's an emergency, it is better to talk to the person live than leave multiple panicked messages.

If you are swamped and your phone keeps ringing:

- If you have caller ID, screen your calls and only answer the ones from key clients and superiors.

- If you have an assistant, use him to screen calls for you. Coach him with an acceptable message. "Keisha is expecting your call and will call you back as soon as possible."

- Don't answer the phone if you are talking with someone at your desk about a business-related matter, unless you are expecting an urgent call. If you do take the call, explain to the person at your desk that the call is important.

Visit Vault at www.vault.com for insider company profiles, expert advice, career message boards, expert resume reviews, the Vault Job Board and more.

VAULT CAREER LIBRARY   59

- Use the "send to voice mail" (also known as "Do Not Disturb") function on your phone. Consult your phone system manual to find out how to activate the feature.

- Turn the ringer off.

- Go to the company's conference room, library or café to finish your work.

- Return calls when you think the other person will not be there: at lunch, nonstandard business hours, weekends and so on. (If you are calling a workaholic, however, this can backfire!)

Meeting Skills

Being nervous before a meeting is a sign that you may not have prepared enough. You should be comfortable expressing your thoughts and participating in discussion – though this is often easier said than done. Women are especially prone to have an overactive self-censoring mechanism, where they do not voice their opinions and ideas because they're "not good enough."

Remind yourself that you have been invited to participate in a call or meeting because you are seen to have something to contribute on that topic. Your silence during these discussions will cause colleagues or clients who may not interact with you regularly to question your intelligence and value, and you run the risk of not being invited next time. At the same time, do not say something just to say something – babbling is just as bad as silence.

Tough love

Moments before walking into a meeting, a boss turned to a young subordinate and stated, "I want you to say two smart things in this meeting." The boss had lost patience with the young employee, who cranked out brilliant work back in the office but remained silent in front of the client as if he did not know a thing. Of course, the employee was stressed out by the mandate, both the quota and the criteria that his remarks qualify as "smart," but it was a tough-love order that got him used to talking in front of others.

Give yourself the same type of ultimatum before you walk into a meeting – the more you pretend you are confident about your contributions, the more you will actually shed your insecurities. Here are some ways to fake confidence – until you actually become confident!

- Organize your thoughts before you open your mouth. If you make points in a scatter-gun fashion, people are more likely to tune you out.

- Force yourself to speak slowly, loudly and clearly for maximum impact.

- Keep your emotions in check in your professional communications. Be prepared for people to argue with you or even become angry. Do not lose your temper. You will look unprofessional. Instead, make sure you understand the points and calmly refute them.

- The more data you have supporting your position, the more confident you will feel in expressing your thoughts, and the more credibility you will have. If you do not have appropriate data in front of you, however, do not apologize for its absence. Tell the group you will distribute the key documents as soon as you get back to your office.

- Generally, do not take subjective differences of opinion personally. You should always feel comfortable participating in the discussion, even if your ideas are not ultimately used. If you find yourself constantly overruled or silenced, however, assess with your confidantes or your manager how to develop a more effective approach to getting your opinions heard and accepted. Your style of delivery is just as important as your message.

- Think before you talk. Ask yourself whether your thought adds value to the discussion. Talkers who extend the length of meetings for no reason are often disliked.

If you are attending a meeting:

- Get the agenda in advance, if possible, so you can be prepared for all the discussion topics.

- Know your role before a meeting or call and contribute accordingly (e.g., observer, participant, presenter, advocate, moderator, note taker, etc.). If you are the note taker, make sure you can read and understand your notes so that you can quickly type them up and distribute them.

- Bring these basics to a meeting:

  – pen

  – paper

  – calculator

  – calendar, to schedule follow-up meetings

Visit Vault at **www.vault.com** for insider company profiles, expert advice, career message boards, expert resume reviews, the Vault Job Board and more.

VAULT CAREER LIBRARY   61

— business cards, for when you are meeting new people

— any handouts, if you are or your team is, responsible for their production

Here are some other ways to make meetings work for you.

- Be punctual.

- Make sure you doublecheck the meeting location. Check your e-mail and voice mail right before the meeting in case of last minute time or location changes. Bring call-in numbers for conference calls.

- Leave some buffer time before your next appointment, because meetings typically run late.

- Take copious notes in meetings, including:

  — names of attendees
  — who says what
  — list of open items or issues raised to address

- Review and clarify your notes immediately after the meeting while the information is still fresh in your mind. File them where you can find them again.

If you are coordinating (or leading) a meeting:

- Confirm with your manager the need for the meeting, when it should be held, how urgent the meeting is, agenda items and projected meeting length.

- Prepare and distribute an agenda in advance of the meeting (more than a day is ideal) so that participants have time to prepare. Bring extra copies of the agenda to the meeting. Don't expect people to remember to bring them.

- Base the time for the meeting on the schedule of the most senior attendees.

- If one or two people's schedules are making scheduling impossible, tell your manager so she can either decide the meeting can be scheduled without them, or ask the busy individuals to clear space on their schedules.

- Reserve a conference room for the meeting, along with all the necessary electronic equipment.

- Distribute an e-mail to participants and their assistants confirming the meeting specifics:

  - time

  - anticipated length

  - place

  - call-in phone number for anyone participating remotely

  - agenda with topics and any presenters clearly noted

- Arrive early to the meeting site. Your team will appreciate your foresight and preparedness, and you will impress people if the meeting actually starts on time with everything working. An early arrival allows you to:

  - Make sure the conference room is available. Even when you have reserved space, you will sometimes find a more important meeting running late and still occupying your space. Have a backup space in mind.

  - Make sure the meeting space is clean. Sometimes meeting rooms are left messy.

  - Make sure the room is equipped for your meeting. Even at technology companies, the projectors and computers rarely work right away, and the meeting organizer generally spends several minutes fiddling with the equipment.

  - Log in and call up your files on your laptop or on a conference room screen.

  - Check the Internet connection if it will be used.

  - Review your materials before a presentation.

  - Retrieve materials you may have forgotten in your office.

  - Make extra copies for unexpected attendees.

Always Have a Backup Plan

When you are in charge of any event, make sure you have a backup plan. Try to anticipate all the problems that can happen with each step and figure out in advance how you will address them.

Visit Vault at **www.vault.com** for insider company profiles, expert advice, career message boards, expert resume reviews, the Vault Job Board and more.

VAULT CAREER LIBRARY

63

If Plan A goes smoothly, you will look like a hero. And if Plan A fails, and you smoothly execute Plan B, you will look like a hero as well. It's a no-lose situation. The safety net is worth the extra investment in time and thought.

Know When to Execute Plan B

Former vice president, business development & information technology, Pallotta TeamWorks

My company produced large-scale charity events for causes ranging from AIDS to breast cancer. These events took the form of multi-day walks and bike rides involving thousands of participants who raise millions of dollars for each cause. At the start of each event, my company needed to register everyone in a timely and organized manner.

We were rolling out new registration software to process the 4,000 participants expected at The Breast Cancer 3-Day Walk in San Diego. Before the event, we were not able to fully test the software system with that volume of registrants. So, during our event preparations, we were careful to devise a backup Plan B in case the new software failed.

On the day of the event, the new software worked smoothly for the first half hour of registration. We were very confident that we had succeeded in developing a flawless system. And then it began to happen. The volunteer computer operators started to raise their hands one by one, the signal to indicate system trouble to our tech team. In minutes, eighty terminals were down and awaiting repair. The new software had malfunctioned, and my team started to work madly to debug it.

The launch of Plan B was put off repeatedly for "just five more minutes" in hopes of successfully fixing Plan A. As every interval of "five more minutes" passed, the line grew from hundreds to thousands of impatient participants. Our goal to register participants in a timely manner had been overshadowed by our goal to get the new software working. By the time we finally abandoned the new software and launched Plan B, 4,000 pissed-off participants had waited in line for up to five hours.

Our foresight in devising Plan B was undermined by our failure to set exact parameters for pulling the trigger on it. We should have specified and strictly observed a set amount of time we would give to fixing Plan A before Plan B would be executed. After all, neither our client charity nor the event participants cared what software we were using to register people; they just wanted the event run efficiently.

Computer Skills

Mastering four basic applications as early as possible in your career will make your work life a lot easier:

- Microsoft Excel for charts, budgets and analyses.

- Microsoft Word for memos, letters and tables.

- Microsoft PowerPoint for presentations.

- Microsoft Outlook to organize your calendar, contacts, e-mail communications, and to schedule meetings.

Don't wait until you are asked to make a PowerPoint presentation to use it for the first time. All of these applications have a vast array of functions and features to help you incorporate shapes, arrows, tables, graphs and formulas into your document. But there are right and wrong ways to format your work. Without exploring the applications and testing the various menu and toolbar options in advance, you will almost certainly put your document together in an inefficient way. Though it may look OK, these inefficiencies will haunt you and waste your time later if you need to scale, copy or change the formatting on an object. Make templates for documents that you will reuse. You will likely revise your documents many times in the course of a project, as well as recycle documents for other projects.

This chapter is not an applications manual, but a list of functions and features that you will need to master if you want to work efficiently.

Microsoft Excel

- Making a table with cells

- Function Wizard

- Chart Wizard

- Drag and drop formulas

- "F4" button to hold either row and/or column number constant when dragging and dropping formulas

- Insert a regression line in a chart (Under "Chart" menu, "Add Trendline")

- Password protection for opening and revising a workbook

Visit Vault at **www.vault.com** for insider company profiles, expert advice, career message boards, expert resume reviews, the Vault Job Board and more.

VAULT CAREER LIBRARY   **65**

- Tools menu "Options" (e.g., "Show formulas" to see the formulas in each cell; "Hide Gridlines" to hide the cell borders when copying a part of an Excel spreadsheet into Word or PowerPoint)

- "Format" menu, "Cells" option (for fonts, borders, etc.)

Important: Set up assumptions at the top of the page or on a separate worksheet, and link subsequent cell formulas to the assumption cells for ease of changing scenarios.

Microsoft Word

- Table function

- Table of Contents function

- Outlining function, including bullets

- Search and replace function

- Advanced search for files

- Tools menu "Options," including redlining function (Track Changes)

- Numbering sections

- Importing Microsoft Excel graphs

- Key Caps to insert specialized symbols and accents

- Paragraph spacing option

Microsoft PowerPoint

- Master slide function for consistent formatting

- Table function

- Graph function

- Shape and arrow drawing (double click on shape to insert text)

- Text boxes

- Importing Microsoft Excel graphs

- Key Caps to insert specialized symbols and accents

Microsoft Outlook

- Out of office assistant (sends out an automatic e-mail letting people know you are out of the office – very helpful for when you are on vacation)

- Calendar (including sending meeting requests and viewing other people's schedules)

- Appointment scheduler

- Contact list

- Advanced search for files

- Recalling sent e-mails. Your intended recipient will be alerted that you recalled a message. This function will not retrieve messages that were opened before your recall attempt.

Samples

Your company will probably have standard forms for letters, memos, agendas, meeting notes, fax cover sheets, and charts. You should ask for these forms when you start work. If your company does not have these standard forms, see Appendix A for some examples.

Controlling Your Work Product

Your work product is part content, part presentation. If you don't present the information in a visually clean, professional, logical format, you immediately lose credibility. Readers may wonder if a spelling error is indicative of logic errors.

It's probably better to format your work as if it were the final product, even when you're doing early drafts. Here's why.

- Your manager and client will have a better sense of your progress and overall vision.

- Everyone will be aware of what content still needs to be provided. (To indicate missing information, include a blank page with a title for a forthcoming slide; write "TBD" or "forthcoming" in the white space for a missing paragraph; insert X's where you intend to fill in numbers, e.g., "The annual return was XX%.")

Visit Vault at **www.vault.com** for insider company profiles, expert advice, career message boards, expert resume reviews, the Vault Job Board and more.

VAULT CAREER LIBRARY   67

- You can review and improve the flow and presentation of the information.

- You avoid last minute time crunches.

- You will have your document spell-checked and cleanly formatted if your manager suddenly pops into your office asking for an interim draft ahead of deadline.

- You won't forget to include the information in the final version.

Make sure your work product:

- is cleanly formatted.

- is ready to print.

- is spell-checked and grammar-checked.

- has numbered pages.

- has titled charts.

- is time/date/file location stamped (particularly important in keeping many iterations of the same document straight).

Have others review important documents before you meet with your client or manager. Fresh eyes are always helpful, especially when you have been working long hours, are tired, and are too close to the document to spot mistakes or areas for improvement.

Keep Your Work on Hand
Sucharita Mulpuru, former Disney analyst

Keep all the paperwork. My manager once gave me copious notes written out on a presentation that included many changes for the next draft. After incorporating the changes, I threw the draft away because it was lots of extra paper on my desk, and I'd made all the changes anyway. Bad idea! The first thing my manager wanted to see the next day was her draft with her notes – she needed to check her draft against mine, and until she saw her draft couldn't be sure of all the comments she'd made. My confession about throwing them out and the janitors taking them away did not go over well.

Business Travel Tips

You may find yourself on business trips early in your career. Usually, your departmental assistant will take care of the traveling team's airplane tickets and hotel accommodations, though sometimes this task will fall to you. Here's how to ensure a successful trip.

Before you leave for a business trip

• Find out from your manager what work materials you are responsible for bringing. Gather and pack all the necessary hard copies of meeting documents and backup data, along with extra copies of the presentation. If this is a heavy load of paper, you may want to consider overnighting the bulk of the materials ahead of time to your hotel or client office if you are certain you can send it early. Always keep a copy of important documents with you in case the sent materials are lost or delayed.

• Save all the documents and related backup needed for your meetings on a laptop. If you do not have one, borrow one from your company's IT department.

• Find out how you are supposed to book your trip. Is there a corporate travel department that you have to use? What kind of budget restrictions do you have?

Be Careful Where You Stay

Austen Parrish, former litigation lawyer at O'Melveny & Myers

I had only been at O'Melveny for a short period of time when I was sent to San Francisco to sit in a large arbitration proceeding attended by two partners of my law firm and senior executives of our client, a *Fortune* 500 company. Before going up to San Francisco, I called our travel department to make hotel reservations.

Originally, they suggested a room at the Mandarin Oriental (a whopping $400/night). I told them I wanted something reasonable. So they told me the best deal they had was The Ritz at about $230/night. Everything else was said to be sold out. Sounded good to me, so I took it! When I got to the Ritz, they put me up in an Executive Suite –

Visit Vault at **www.vault.com** for insider company profiles, expert advice, career message boards, expert resume reviews, the Vault Job Board and more.

VAULT CAREER LIBRARY   69

essentially a three room Taj Mahal (two TVs, two bathrooms/one with a small jacuzzi, a meeting area, bedroom, and changing room).

The next morning, the partner of my law firm left me a message to meet him at his hotel. Turns out The Ritz was not the only hotel with rooms available. The partners and the client had been put up at the Holiday Inn – at approximately $150/night. There were lots of vacancies there. The rooms were the equivalent of a Motel 6 and, to make matters worse, there was a lot of construction going on – they had been awakened in the morning to the tune of jack hammers.

Of course, the first thing I was asked by the tired-looking senior partner: "So, Austen, where did you stay last night?" No matter how you phrase it, "The Ritz" is not a great answer. I thought my days were numbered after that one... When one of the partners stopped by my suite, which was twice the size of his "Holiday Inn Special," I was so embarrassed. For my next trip, I checked to see where the partners had booked first!

- Print out a detailed list of important contact information: cell phone numbers for your teammates, phone numbers and addresses for your hotel, client offices and any restaurants where you have reservations.

- Print out relevant Internet maps and directions.

- Confirm a meeting time and place with your teammates. Are you meeting at the office to carpool to the airport, or at the airport? If you are meeting at the airport, are you meeting at the ticket counter, at the gate or in the airline's business travelers' club?

- Plan to arrive at the meeting site or at the airport 30 minutes earlier than your meeting time, in case you get stuck in traffic, need to get a snack or have to make a last minute run to the ATM.

What to bring

Only pack carry-on luggage. Never check any bag if you can help it. Sometimes client meetings are scheduled just hours after you land, so there is no time to wait for your bags to arrive on the luggage carousel. Even worse, you don't want to risk losing your meeting materials if your luggage doesn't make the right flight.

To bring:

• Ticket

• Photo ID

• Passport, if you are flying outside the country

• Frequent flier numbers for airline, hotel and rental car credit

• Credit cards

• Plenty of cash, for parking, cabs, tips and the occasional snack

• List of important contact information

• Directions to hotel, client offices, etc., and any key phone numbers

• Meeting materials and backup data

• Granola bar and bottle of water, in case you need an energy boost before a meeting

• Standard business meeting basics (business cards, pen and paper, calculator, personal calendar, etc.)

Carry-on luggage:

• Toiletry kit

• Travel alarm clock

• Business clothes: daily change of shirts, underwear, and socks; one or two basic suits and dress shoes you can re-wear

• Some business casual clothes, in case the client hosts an activity after work hours

• Workout clothes, if you want to take advantage of the hotel gym

• Sleepwear

Take care of your belongings

Try to consolidate everything in as few bags as possible so they are easy to transport and remember. If you are loaded down with a separate briefcase, purse, winter coat, laptop bag and file boxes, it is very likely you will forget something in a cab or restaurant.

Visit Vault at **www.vault.com** for insider company profiles, expert advice, career message boards, expert resume reviews, the Vault Job Board and more.

VAULT CAREER LIBRARY   71

Using your expense account

Many companies have a travel policy itemizing what employees can and cannot be reimbursed for. If your company doesn't have a policy, check with your manager about your company's expense account parameters.

Be careful to keep all of your receipts while you are traveling, so you don't get stuck paying for something because you lost the receipt. Make sure to ask for receipts from cab drivers and other vendors who may not automatically give you a receipt. Keep track of cash tips you hand out to cab drivers, hotel staff and restaurant servers, and write the amounts on the bottom of the relevant receipts for your complete reimbursement.

What is acceptable to expense? During the workday, you will be expensing transportation costs between the hotel and work sites, as well as any business meals you are taking with clients or colleagues. Any side trips you take to see friends should be paid for out of your own pocket (although it is usually OK for you to use the rental car for this purpose if no one else needs it). At the hotel, it is usually acceptable to expense a few long distance calls home and to the office, room service for a simple breakfast or evening meal, the daily fee for use of the gym, dry cleaning (only if you are staying for several days and need clean work clothes) and an occasional pay-per-view movie at night if you need to relax after a long day.

Your expenditures should be comparable with the moderate expenses you would be incurring on your own at home. Don't go crazy and try to expense filet mignon and expensive wines that you would never order on your own dime. You may have to pay for it yourself when your manager sees your expense report. Of course if your manager explicitly tells you to treat yourself to a spa visit or a bottle of champagne because the project went so well, don't be shy!

In flight

You may be expected to work on the plane, especially if you are sitting next to a superior and traveling during business hours. Don't assume you can sleep or watch the in-flight movie. Prepare work for the flight. However, you can take your cue from your highest-level colleagues on the trip – if the partner is chatting, reading a novel or napping, then you can too.

At the hotel

Always ask the hotel for a wake-up call and set the in-room alarm clock. Set the alarm with plenty of time to spare. Eat breakfast before a morning meeting so you are not sleepy or hungry. It's difficult to eat at a business meeting, especially if you will be talking a lot.

On the job

Jet lag can be a pain. If you can schedule some buffer time before you have to get into the office or a meeting, do so. Do not volunteer to go straight in. If you have to, realize your limitations induced by travel. One new consultant was called into the client's office after flying from California to Belgium. Because he did not get enough sleep, he stumbled through some basic project work and nearly undid a month of preparation. He had to spend the rest of his two weeks there proving that he truly did know what he was doing!

After business hours

Don't assume you'll have the evening off. You may be expected to work late with the clients or with your team in order to have materials prepared for the next day. If you don't need to work all night, you may be expected to dine with the clients or with your team while you are on a business trip. Meals are a great opportunity to build on your positive working relationship with your colleagues or your clients.

If you have friends or family you want to visit in town, make sure you find out from your manager when you have free time in the schedule. Your manager will let you know if it is OK to excuse yourself from after-hours work obligations for personal reasons. It's probably best to have your friends meet you at the hotel for a quick drink – even if the client dinner is "optional," it's much better to go than not.

Visit Vault at **www.vault.com** for insider company profiles, expert advice, career message boards, expert resume reviews, the Vault Job Board and more.

VAULT CAREER LIBRARY   **73**

Business Trip Conduct After Hours
Former strategic planning analyst

In your first job after college, business trips seem exciting for a number of nonprofessional reasons: free food, swank hotels, frequent flier miles and a chance to see friends in another city. Lucky me, my first business trip was overseas. I was looking forward to the opportunity to reconnect with an old flame. After a grueling trip and a long day of meetings, I raced back to my hotel for a romantic night of dinner and drinks. Way too much wine was consumed.

The next day of meetings was a complete nightmare. I was hung over and nodding off at the conference table – my notes showed my handwriting trailing off as I dozed. Later, someone heard me getting sick in the bathroom. I tried to pass my illness off as food poisoning. Back home, my boss called me into his office and asked me how I was feeling. I again used the food poisoning excuse, but I could tell he saw right through it. He generously let me slink out of his office, but his unsaid message was clear: a business trip is business 24 hours a day.

Heading home

If you accumulate more papers during your trip than you can fit in your luggage, ask your client or hotel to FedEx your work materials back to your office for you. (Make sure you get your manager's approval beforehand.)

Special caution: Travel relationships

Out of the office, far from your routine lives, you may find yourself and your colleagues sharing more personal interactions. Certain colleagues, who are usually tied down with a significant other or a family after work, may take advantage of business trips as an opportunity to cut loose with partying, drinking, flirtation, even infidelity. Some companies go by the mantra, "What goes on the road, stays on the road."

Be careful. Don't think you've suddenly made new, fabulous friends with your co-workers. You don't want to confide anything you'll later regret. And you don't want to hear anyone else's confidences you can't keep back in the office! If you do engage in "airplane pillow talk" with a colleague about people or issues back in the office or in your personal lives, make sure you are clear that certain remarks are confidential, and keep it that way!

Business travel does provide an intimate opportunity for you, a lowly new hire, to network with superiors. However, be careful about flirtations that can develop with colleagues during a business trip. Don't be naïve; make the distinction between desirable professional attention and inappropriate personal attention from a colleague, and resist the "flattery" of a colleague's inappropriate advances. Compromising your career and dignity for a fling with a married partner is not worth it.

Safety

If you are working late hours, you may find yourself in an unfamiliar environment. Be aware of your surroundings and the people around you, whether with a colleague you know well or people you encounter while traveling. The common sense safety rules still apply: don't give out personal information to people you don't know, don't explore a big city alone at night, don't get rides with people you don't know, and so on. Ask male colleagues to walk you to your hotel room or down isolated streets. It is hard to remember to be safe when you are tired from working late, but that is exactly when you are most vulnerable.

Trust Your Instincts!
Former management consultant

I had a car service driver, who frequently picked me up from the airport, who made me feel a bit uncomfortable. I was concerned I was being too sensitive even though he always tried to chat me up and everything he said was slightly inappropriate. One time, he brought me roses, and that was it! I called the car company the next day and let them know it was inappropriate behavior. I did not want the driver to drive me again, and I wanted them to speak to all their drivers about working with women clients. I'd wish I had said something at the first signs of his flirtation.

Visit Vault at **www.vault.com** for insider company profiles, expert advice, career message boards, expert resume reviews, the Vault Job Board and more.

V/\ULT CAREER LIBRARY   75

Evaluations

The review process is part and parcel of a corporate career. A standard evaluation outlines the array of skills and characteristics needed to succeed in your current position and to advance to the next level. Your performance is rated in each category, and normally you are given examples of both good and bad behavior. While no one likes to hear about her flaws and weaknesses, it is essential to view the criticism as constructive and instructive to advancing your professional development. The review is used to determine raises and promotions. If you are not performing up to standards, you will be informed of this fact in the review.

Getting Evaluated

You should understand how your performance will be evaluated since your promotions, salary increases and bonuses are impacted by your performance marks.

When you start your job, ask your boss for details on the evaluation process, including:

- Copies of official evaluation forms.

- Performance measurement criteria.

- Frequency of review. Will you be evaluated quarterly, annually or after each project is completed?

- Sources of input. Who will be asked to contribute opinions on your performance? Clients, superiors, peers and subordinates are all possibilities.

- Correlation to salary increases and bonus. Is it a formulaic correlation (e.g., you receive a weighted performance evaluation of 95%, so you receive 95% of your target bonus) or is it discretionary (e.g., your boss picks a number)?

Maintain your own performance file

Save e-mails. Document (transcribe and date) voice mails that praise your work and send them at review time to your manager. Keep your own running

Visit Vault at **www.vault.com** for insider company profiles, expert advice, career message boards, expert resume reviews, the Vault Job Board and more.

VAULT CAREER LIBRARY

77

list of your strengths and weaknesses and constantly work on shortening the weakness list. Document examples of both sides of the list.

CYA

You should also create a CYA file (Cover Your Ass). This file should include copies of e-mails authorizing decisions, background materials on research, logs of conversations and anything else that you can use to prove you were working with the best information you had and with the best of intentions. Pray that you will never need to use it at a review.

Protect Yourself
Siobhan Green, project manager

I was working as a research assistant for a VP on a big market research contract. Even though I had just joined, it became pretty clear that the VP didn't know how to manage the research or get the sort of information our client expected, mainly because it didn't exist. He had oversold what we could deliver and refused to acknowledge this fact to the client.

I worked very hard, but found little or no relevant information on the topic from the very beginning. A co-worker mentioned that I needed to make sure to document the updates I was giving the VP via e-mail, which I did. Every day, I sent him an update of my work and made sure the e-mails were time stamped when I came in very early or stayed very late. I also kept his responses, which proved that he had been aware of the situation all along.

When we delivered the project to the client, they were furious at the lack of real data, and walked out the door. The VP needed someone to blame – and I was a convenient scapegoat. Luckily I got a copy of his e-mail, blaming me entirely for the loss of the client. I pulled out my CYA file, walked into my supervisor's office to prove that the VP had known all along about my problems, and that I had been asking for more guidance and suggestions for over a month. She was able to take my file to our president to convince him not to fire me immediately. (The VP ended up leaving soon thereafter to "spend more time with his family.")

> **Important:** A CYA file is essential if there is anything potentially illegal or immoral going on. Keep a file that clearly documents that dubious decisions were not made by you but by your supervisor or others, and that you alerted others to any questionable actions. Look at the recent Enron and Arthur Andersen scandals – employees with clear documentation that they acted under direct orders or alerted senior staff to improprieties found themselves able to avoid prosecution. You should not be held responsible for someone else's lack of ethical judgment.

Communication is key

Communicate regularly with your boss, your team and your clients to make sure your performance meets their expectations. At the end of important projects, ask for their feedback on your strengths and weaknesses, and strive to improve upon those weaknesses during your next project together. Some companies regularly have "post mortems" to review how a project went. Feel free to schedule time with your manager to get feedback if you don't think you will be able to get the information in a meeting, over lunch or a chat in the hallways. You can ask for comments on your performance in a nonthreatening way: "I'd like to make sure the next project runs even more smoothly than this one, so it'd be great if you could give me some feedback now." Your formal reviews should not be a surprise to you, but an accumulation of the informal feedback you have gotten all year long.

Before you are reviewed, you may be asked to fill out a self-assessment form. Your co-workers and managers will also be asked to fill out a form that evaluates your performance. Do not be modest. If you've done well, don't be shy about saying so. Your peers are likely overestimating their own performance.

Your performance at the end of the year (or evaluation period) will probably influence the evaluating sources' remarks most heavily. If you are regularly checking in with your manager and adjusting your performance over the course of the year, it is likely that a weak start to the year will be forgotten by the time you sit down to your formal review. If you end the year on a down note, arm yourself with evidence from your earlier projects to remind your reviewer that you are a high-quality employee.

Visit Vault at **www.vault.com** for insider company profiles, expert advice, career message boards, expert resume reviews, the Vault Job Board and more.

VAULT CAREER LIBRARY   79

Communicate With Your Boss About Your Performance

Strategic planning analyst

Be proactive when managing your career, and don't be scared of asking direct, pointed questions about your performance and your chances of promotion. I was in a job once where I never received a performance evaluation. I was there for two years and got two annual raises with my peers.

After the second year, my peers and I were all slated to get promoted to senior analysts – the next level up. There was supposed to be an official ceremony, but I hadn't heard anything about it. I figured that my boss was just a little flaky and forgot to mention it to me. I showed up at the ceremony in front of our entire department where everyone's name, except mine, was announced as being promoted.

At the time, I thought it was an oversight. It turned out that it wasn't. Over coffee the next week, my boss apologized for not making time to talk with me earlier, and she was sorry that I found out in a public forum. I just wasn't delivering what she expected.

All of this was a surprise to me as I'd never received this feedback before. In retrospect, she was an atrocious manager, but my biggest mistake was that I didn't insist on more conversations with her along the way; that I didn't ask her directly what I could be doing better; that I didn't ask what she didn't like about the work I was doing; and, most of all, that I never asked point-blank if I would be promoted based on my work.

Your review will normally consist of a relatively brief meeting with your manager. Occasionally, an HR representative will be present as well. Sometimes you will receive copies of your evaluations. If you do not receive these copies, ask for them.

When you receive your review:

• Contain your emotions.

• View negative feedback as a challenge and an opportunity to improve yourself and learn more.

• Accept positive feedback graciously and remember to say, "Thanks!"

- Defer response until you have organized your thoughts. Schedule time with your manager to discuss your response, so that you have time to read and digest the feedback.

- Make sure your manager has documented specific and representative successes and failures. Do not accept a vaguely negative criticism without reference to specific projects or actions. The reviewers have to be accurate, specific and accountable for their remarks.

- Share specific examples proving your perspective if you disagree. Bring your own performance file as backup. Your CYA file will come in handy if there is a disagreement.

- Pick your battles. If you are happy with your review overall, it is not worth arguing over subjective feedback about one specific area. Accept minor criticisms like, "You should read more about the industry." Those comments are usually made because the reviewer has nothing really bad to say but must come up with some constructive criticism.

Learn from your review

- Listen closely to your reviews. While you may not agree with all of it, at least recognize your perceived weaknesses. Think of ways to not only fix the weakness, but also the perception of weakness.

- Know your strengths and weaknesses, and actively manage your weaknesses. It doesn't matter if you are not comfortable with a certain skill, or it takes you a little longer to accomplish something in a particular area, as long as you get to the point where the end result is solid and timely. The worst thing you can do is ignore your weaknesses.

- Approach role models. Get advice from people who are strong in areas where you are weak.

- Observe superstars. You do not have to have a personal relationship with role models to learn from them.

- Keep improving yourself. Skill and intuition can be developed with discipline, determination and patience.

- If you got a great review, stay humble. No new employee knows everything. If you become arrogant, people will wait for you to fail and will jump on your first mistake. If a peer asks you how you did, be positive but vague. Never discuss a raise or bonus. Others may not have received pay increases.

Visit Vault at **www.vault.com** for insider company profiles, expert advice, career message boards, expert resume reviews, the Vault Job Board and more.

VAULT CAREER LIBRARY   **81**

Managing Relationships

How you interact with the people you meet in and out of the office will directly affect your career path. This chapter outlines the critical contingencies you will come across during your workday and how to approach each.

Establish Important Office Relationships

Eric Keene, former McKinsey consultant

I was told by a partner at McKinsey that the three things you need to have in place to be successful (at a professional services firm) are:

1) A senior/executive-level champion who speaks on your behalf in closed door sessions.

2) Someone senior to you who's willing to coach you.

3) At least one peer, or ideally a few peers, to whom you can occasionally bitch about your organization behind closed doors in a risk-free environment.

If you don't have all three in place, or aren't on your way to achieving these three things within a year, chances are you will not be successful at that organization.

Visit Vault at **www.vault.com** for insider company profiles, expert advice, career message boards, expert resume reviews, the Vault Job Board and more.

VAULT CAREER LIBRARY

83

Anne-Marie Nuñez, a former market researcher, divided her clients into quadrants, and developed strategies for dealing with each type of person. Her analysis can be applied to co-workers and managers

	Dumb	Smart
Nice	These people are benign and easy to please. You won't learn much, but they won't stress you out either. They'll never challenge your work, or find a mistake in it.	You will learn a lot from these people. They will challenge you to grow professionally. Try to align yourself with them and emulate them.
Mean	The worst combination for causing you stress and frustration. Give them what they want, and make them feel important. Generally, steer clear if you can!	Try to learn from them, and don't take any caustic remarks personally. Learn what makes them lash out. Then avoid setting them off.

Social Skills are Key

Victor Hwang, former corporate lawyer, current COO LARTA (a nonprofit think tank)

I learned some of my best lessons from watching a co-worker at my law firm. He was from a successful family and was a fun-loving fraternity type. After a while, it was clear that he was not necessarily that much brighter than anyone else, and he obviously did not work harder than many. Still, he ended up working with the best partners on the best projects, worked fairly normal hours and was regarded as being quite competent.

His key was that he endeared himself to people. He used his social skills to position himself favorably within the firm. While others kept their noses to the grindstone, he kept a balanced attitude and played the social game, which made his professional game that much more successful. I copied his actions and over time I found that I was working on better projects, working better hours and was held in higher regard. The social game is just as important as the work itself.

Managing Your Managers

It is not enough to do good work. Your relationship with your manager can make or break your career. The ideal manager:

- Champions and supports you. Your manager should help you rise in the company, teach you a lot, tell others your worth and protect you from bad projects or others' wrath (especially when you make a mistake). You will need your manager's help to get good projects, training, promotions and perks.

- Has power in the office hierarchy. A manager who backs you but has no power or respect from his superiors will not be an effective champion. Get a sense of your manager's power. For example, see how many of your manager's protegés were promoted in the last few years.

Here's how to ensure a good relationship with your manager:

- **Find out exactly what your job is.** Make sure you know exactly what the boss expects from you, at what rate and what hours you should be working, and what the standard review process is.

- **Be explicit about what you need** from your manager in order to perform your job well and with the best attitude. You cannot expect your manager to read your mind. You will probably be more successful getting what you want from your boss if you are clear and upbeat. "Thanks for letting me sit in on that meeting – I learned X, Y, and Z from it. Please let me know if there are more opportunities like that in the future."

- **Review new assignments** with your manager to make sure you understand the project, its desired result, the timeline and the project's priority. Don't make assumptions about the significance of a request until you get the facts straight. If you don't want to barrage your boss with questions, tell her what you think the assignment is. "I'll get you a two-page draft memo on California trade secret law by Wednesday; let me know if you want a final draft sooner." If you're wrong, your boss will correct you.

Visit Vault at **www.vault.com** for insider company profiles, expert advice, career message boards, expert resume reviews, the Vault Job Board and more.

VAULT CAREER LIBRARY   85

Do Your Homework about Your Assignment

Chad Goldman, director of marketing, USA Wireless Solutions

I was working for a computer services company in Argentina for four years as a marketing manager. I used conversational and basic business Spanish in my job daily. One day my boss mentioned in passing, "Oh, Chad, there are some clients coming from Ireland tomorrow. Would you mind doing some Spanish-English translation for them?" I agreed without a second thought.

The next day I walked into a room to find a team of four Ericsson executives facing a team of five Irish clients at a long conference table. I was surprised at the formality of the room for such a "casual" meeting. The Irish team promptly launched into a very technical conversation about their ERP software product. I could hardly understand their thick Irish accents, never mind the fact that I did not know how to say a lot of the technical terms in Spanish! At the end of each sentence both teams turned to look at me, obviously expecting the smooth simultaneous translation of a U.N. interpreter. I stuttered and stumbled and eked my way through the discussion by the skin of my teeth.

As the meeting seemed to wrap up, I felt relieved that it was over. The two teams at the table, on the other hand, were completely agitated and anxiously conferring amongst themselves. I didn't understand the tension. We all stood up and exited the conference room through a different set of doors than we had entered ... and walked into an auditorium filled with a seated audience of 1,000 people! I was escorted to one end of the stage to a podium outfitted with a microphone and reading light. The Irish team walked up to a second podium at the other end of the stage. Between us a formal presentation was projected onto a massive screen. I was absolutely mortified!

The Irish speaker began a formal technical presentation of their software. Again, I started stuttering and stumbling in my attempt to first understand the thickly-accented English, and then translate into Spanish. About ten minutes into the presentation, the fatal blow was dealt. In Spanish the words for "Swedish" and "Swiss" are very similar. I made the mistake of calling Ericsson a 'Swiss' company. The team of Ericsson engineers in the audience started booing me! Shortly thereafter, a company executive walked up to me, and escorted me to an open seat in the audience. I had been fired as the interpreter.

As I sat in the audience completely humiliated, I prayed to God to teleport me out of the room. Of course, I would have never agreed to serve as a translator had my boss described the full extent of the responsibility. I had assumed her nonchalance in making the request to mean I would be interpreting for two guys in a room casually shooting the breeze! This public humiliation taught me a major lesson in asking detailed questions about ambiguous assignments before accepting them.

- **Meet your deadlines.** Monitor your progress by finding out in advance how much time your manager and your more experienced peers expect you to spend on each step of the work plan. If you are falling behind schedule, let your manager know right away so that you can get the guidance or extra resources you need to get back on track. If you are certain you are going to blow a deadline even with extra guidance, inform your manager immediately without whining about it. Don't make excuses, even if they are valid. Instead, let her know the revised timeline and how you are resolving the problem(s).

- **Give your manager something to react to** if you want guidance. Outline your work steps to your manager to get feedback (e.g., "What do you think of these work steps?"), rather than asking for open-ended advice (e.g., "What should I do?") If your manager is strapped for time, it's easier for her to assess your plan instead of creating ideas from scratch for you. Also, unless you are completely new, your manager will expect some proactive effort and thinking on your part. You can ask peers to look over your plans before you meet with your manager to make sure you are not completely off base.

- **Check in with progress updates without being asked.** You don't get extra credit for working without your manager's guidance; on the contrary, things could go awry if you try to play the hero and do everything by yourself. You could head down the wrong path for days or weeks, wasting your time and the time of others depending on your work.

- **Anticipate your manager's questions and requests** and try to preemptively provide responses. One part of being good at your job is learning what your boss wants. Typically, people have consistent work

Visit Vault at **www.vault.com** for insider company profiles, expert advice, career message boards, expert resume reviews, the Vault Job Board and more.

VAULT CAREER LIBRARY

87

styles and thought processes. You will earn your boss's confidence if she doesn't have to ask you the same questions every time.

- **When you get feedback that you disagree with, discuss the facts,** not your opinions, with your boss. If it's a matter of style, accept your boss's opinion.

- **Collect questions for your manager during the day and ask them all at once at a regular interval.** Don't ask your manager each new question that pops into your mind at that moment. Your manager will appreciate your respect for her time.

- **Know who needs to review and approve your work.** You could have multiple managers on one project. Keep them updated on each other's instructions to you and have them review your work before it's finalized to make sure they are in agreement on all points. You don't want to be the scapegoat because of their lack of communication.

- **Create regular status reports for your manager.** Find out what works best for your manager. Does she want daily status reports, or will a weekly or twice-monthly report do? Does she prefer e-mail, a five-page memo, or would she rather meet with you a few days a week?

Challenging Your Boss in a Nonthreatening Way
Lisa Strick, marketing executive

One important lesson I learned is to never cause your boss to lose face in a meeting. When a senior executive suggested something that I believed was incorrect or would have undesirable results, I used to state exactly what I was thinking. But my blunt comments would turn the conversation into a power play instead of a constructive exchange of ideas. I learned that the best way to get my thoughts and ideas heard was to put off my comments to a later private conversation.

My new strategy was to respond to questionable suggestions from senior executives with "That's an alternative we haven't looked into. Give me some time to think about how we can make it work, and let me get back to you." Then, at a later time, I would bring up the subject, without attributing ownership to the manager, mention the reasons why it wouldn't work and suggest something else. It was a very successful approach.

The key to remember: when you challenge your boss's ideas, it is not perceived as input or critical thinking but just as a challenge.

When your manager is on vacation

To avoid disaster, you should talk to your managers before they leave the office about how to handle work in their absence. Be clear on what you're supposed to do in their absence. Do you have added responsibilities? Whom are you supporting? What is due when? What are the parameters of your decision-making? Whom should you consult if you have questions? What contact, if any, should you have with clients? What are the emergency contact numbers?

Things to do when your boss is away

- Consult with others about key decisions. Don't try to be the hero and solve all problems yourself. While you could look good in the end, you risk screwing things up because of a lack of complete information. You are part of a team for a reason; collaborate with your colleagues.

- Keep your manager informed by copying him on e-mail. Find out if your manager wants faxes or deliveries when away.

- Record your activities and why you did what you did so you can brief your manager upon his return.

Managing Laterally/Downwards: Peers/Staff/Subordinates

You don't need to get to know everyone around the office well in order to have a great reputation as a nice and smart person. All it takes is a little effort to smile and make small talk. Don't feel pressured to be best friends with everyone. You only need a handful of truly close office relationships.

Foster positive personal interaction

Maintain friendly relationships with everyone around the office with whom you work on projects, regardless of their position and what you think of them personally. Do not burn any bridges. Making friends in the trenches (assistants and support people) is especially critical for getting administrative help when you need it in a crunch.

- Don't take people for granted, even if what they do for you is part of their job.

Visit Vault at **www.vault.com** for insider company profiles, expert advice, career message boards, expert resume reviews, the Vault Job Board and more.

V/\ULT CAREER LIBRARY   **89**

- Remember names and personal details about your co-workers.

- Bring something into the office once in a while – a box of donuts for the kitchen, or small gifts from your vacation for department members or teammates.

- Be discreet with what you say in the office. Your co-workers are different from your friends, and having positive work relationships is different from having good friendships. Your co-workers are less likely to share your interests, have little to gain from protecting you and may ultimately be competing against you!

Don't Burn Bridges with Co-workers
Reporter at a large media company

I am an Ivy League grad with professional degrees who has worked at two main jobs, both of which have subjected me to a revolving door of different bosses. In both jobs, I've also worked with lots of other colleagues who could influence my performance evaluations and future job assignments, even though I didn't report to them. One of the most important lessons I've learned is the delicate line between being the best that I can be, and not offending or bruising the egos of others as I climb ahead.

I've been told multiple times that some people, even those with more seniority than I, can feel intimidated or threatened by me. Three years ago, I made the mistake of arguing with one of those people in a way that inadvertently belittled him. At the time I thought he was an idiot and of little consequence to me. But a few weeks later, my run-in with him found its way into my performance review, to my surprise. And today, that same man has become my direct boss!

Now when I have professional disagreements with him, I smile sweetly even as I grit my teeth. I pick my battles and approach unavoidable conflicts in a diplomatic and constructive way that doesn't threaten his ego. I schmooze him and his family all I can. The good news is that I have come to like him and respect his strengths.

I learned an invaluable lesson to be friendly and respectful to everyone I work with, no matter if it's the CEO or the secretary down the hall, because you never know when something will come back to harm you.

The corporate world values teamwork. Here are some tips on working well with your peers.

- Good communication is vital. Share information with teammates – the timeline, what you're doing, what resources you're using – to prevent duplicated efforts.

- When making a last minute request of someone, especially someone who has not been working on the project all along, take the time to explain how the requested piece fits into the big picture. The perspective gives the person a sense of contribution to the team, and makes him more enthusiastic about assisting you. For example, if you have to ask an administrative assistant to stay after normal business hours and help you type cover letters and prepare packages being mailed out to the client the next day, try to avoid "ordering" him to do it. Apologize for the short notice, and take the time to explain whom the project is for, how the deadline was moved up a day and what pieces of the package you still need to prepare, so his contribution in typing the letters and preparing the packages will be critical to meeting the deadline.

- Offer your help when others are swamped and you have free time, and be prepared to follow through. Whether your offer is accepted or not, you will win brownie points for your good teamwork.

- Make sure you thank people at the end of the project, both by e-mail and in person.

Managing Your Clients

One of the interesting aspects of working in the client service industry is the constant rotation of new clients in and out of your world. These are the people who ultimately pay your salary, so you must establish a positive working relationship with them.

You will be able to meet interesting people and learn about different industries and companies through your interaction with your clients. If you do a good job, it is very possible one of your future job opportunities will come from a client contact. If you don't do a good job, or if you don't like a client, at least you can look forward to starting with a clean slate with a new client. But try to minimize the occurrence of the latter! If you continually clash with clients, you'll probably find yourself out of a job sooner rather than later.

Visit Vault at **www.vault.com** for insider company profiles, expert advice, career message boards, expert resume reviews, the Vault Job Board and more.

VAULT CAREER LIBRARY   **91**

Know what your clients expect from you

- How does the client want to stay in touch? Do they want a memo detailing your work? A teleconference? A face to face meeting? An e-mail?

- Get samples of past work for the client, if possible. Even if it's not on the same subject, you can see the structure, layout and level of detail your client wants.

Always Deliver Bad News
Kristi Anderson, executive recruiter, TMP Worldwide

Never delay or fail to deliver bad news. If you communicate with your clients regularly, then you will always have good and bad news to update them. The bad news won't be such a big deal, just part of doing business. If you don't communicate with clients regularly enough, it is much harder and more daunting to place a special call just to discuss bad news.

Respond to clients' requests as soon as possible, and by no later than the end of the business day. If you don't have the answer, tell them when you will have it. Do not tell your clients that their requests are ridiculous. If you think boundaries have been crossed, talk to your manager.

Your job will be easier if you schmooze your clients. People love to talk about themselves. An easy icebreaker is to ask what they like about their work, or what they like to do outside of work. If they have kids, then learn about them – everyone loves to talk about their kids.

If you hate your client and the project is not ending anytime soon, remind yourself that pretending you like them is an excellent challenge for your own professional development. You will come across all kinds of clients in your career, and you have to remind yourself that they are paying for your salary and professional training until you can move onto something bigger and better.

When having issues with a client, maintain an impersonal perspective. Often people are not reacting to you out of spite; they have other problems and they're taking it out on you.

The only exception to this rule is if the client is personally abusive or prejudiced toward you. If the client is making improper sexual advances toward you or discussing your ethnicity in a deprecating manner, speak to your manager and log your complaints. Work with your manager to be taken off the assignment.

Dealing with Difficult Clients
Anne-Marie Nuñez, former market researcher

I had one such client who was incredibly frustrating. Once, my contact there called me up, screaming at me over the phone. After that initial surge of stress and panic washed over me, I took a deep breath, summoned my most calm, patient and saccharine sweet voice, and turned the questions on her. "What can I do for you? How can I make this right for you?"

My approach made the client feel like she had my full attention, and that I was there just to serve them and make them happy. (A smart and mean client would have immediately picked up the fake and condescending tone of my voice.)

Weeks later I got a call from the same client, who was now thrilled with the results of my work.

Managing Friendships with Colleagues

Office friendships come in different forms. In some cases, your relationship may seem no different from your personal friendships outside of work. You know personal information about each other, you talk and hang out together outside of the office. Other times, the friendships are specifically relegated to the office. You hang out and chat during the workday about personal and work-related issues. Or you share a great rapport and like each other a lot, but know nothing personal about each other.

Work friendships are definitely different from personal friendships. When you are in school, friendships are more black and white. Two people bond over a common interest and both know what they are getting out of the relationship. In the office, your top priority should be performing your job well and moving up in the company. This focused goal necessarily impacts the friendships you make with people around the office.

Blurring the lines of your professional relationship and your personal rapport can lead to unprofessional behavior that will compromise your professional credibility.

Visit Vault at **www.vault.com** for insider company profiles, expert advice, career message boards, expert resume reviews, the Vault Job Board and more.

VAULT CAREER LIBRARY   93

- Don't violate professional standards of confidentiality by discussing your work with each other. If you are found out by management, you could both lose your jobs.

- Respect the reporting relationships underlying your friendships. Your manager is first and foremost your manager and second your friend. Your friendship should not be an obstacle to the professional relationship. Don't take it personally when you don't get a choice project or he offers you constructive criticism about your performance.

- Don't take it personally if a work friend does not want to hang out with you on the weekends.

- It is not your friend's responsibility to help you achieve success or avoid failure. It is not within your friend's power to share confidential information about work. For example, if your department is getting restructured and your job is changing, you can't expect your friend in human resources to tell you secretly before the change is made.

- Allow room for professional disagreements. There are legitimate reasons why you might disagree on a co-worker's performance, the significance of a project, or the strategic vision of the company.

- Don't let a work friendship skew your objective assessment of a colleague's performance for better or for worse. You should not be too protective or forgiving of a work friend who is performing poorly. You are not doing him any favors by covering up his mistakes or contributing positive feedback to his review only because you like him.

- Be discreet about how much information you share with work friends. The other person has no incentive to maintain your confidences as you would expect of a personal friend. Your remarks can reach the wrong ears.

- Avoid becoming too chummy with poor performers or troublemakers.

- Don't be naïve if someone is trying to befriend you in a deliberate and unnatural manner. You should not allow yourself to be enlisted in someone else's political squabble. Be coy if someone seems suspiciously inquisitive about you, your background or your work. You can never predict how someone might use information against you.

Mentors and Networking

CHAPTER 9

Mentors and other contacts are invaluable career aids. A mentor can guide you, defend you and develop you. Your personal networks provide support and knowledge beyond your immediate office. They can get your foot in the door for a great opportunity, and help you overcome obstacles in getting a job, promotion or career change. A study by Catalyst, a group that studies women in the corporate world, tracked 368 women and minorities from 1998 through 2001 and showed strong correlation between being mentored and being promoted.

Mentors

Mentors have several uses. They give you objective advice regarding how to develop your professional skills or career path. They give you the inside scoop on how to deal with your company culture, co-workers or specific professional situations you confront. They are seasoned scouts, guiding you and lighting your path through the wilderness of the corporate world.

It can take patience and a little extra time to get to know someone who is older or in a different stage in life than you. Think about your college experience. The people who got to know professors in order to get plum research projects and glowing recommendations for graduate schools were always the "geeks" who went to office hours and raised their hands in class. A professor would never just suddenly knock on your dorm room door and tell you she wanted to take you under her wing. Well, getting a mentor in the work world is going to require the same deliberate effort on your part.

Identifying potential mentors

Mentors can be found inside or outside your company. Look around your department, your company and the professional business organizations to which you belong. Identify people you really admire with whom you cross paths. Don't limit yourself to obvious choices (e.g., the most popular/powerful executive, the person who had your job before you, the person of the same race or gender as you). Any impressive, intelligent and insightful person you meet can evolve into a future mentor.

Visit Vault at **www.vault.com** for insider company profiles, expert advice, career message boards, expert resume reviews, the Vault Job Board and more.

VAULT CAREER LIBRARY 95

Mentors within the company can help champion or cultivate you. In your company, mentors know all the players, politics and pitfalls. Ideally, they are well respected and secure in their positions. They may be a few rungs up the corporate ladder and can help you understand different managers' personalities and preferred working styles, office politics and the lessons they have learned.

Mentors outside of work provide objectivity. Choose mentors outside of your office who know your personality and have wisdom from a wide range of experiences. Develop relationships with at least one or two people who have no impact on your career to whom you can openly vent, turn to for perspective and ask for candid feedback. You will appreciate their distance when a work issue is too controversial to discuss with a fellow colleague, even in confidence.

In many cases, you may not even need a personal relationship with these people in order to learn from them. Observe their traits from a distance, and emulate them when you get in a position of power. For example, one director at Oracle recalls that he admired a manager who recognized hard work by comping subordinates on expensive dinners and hotel rooms. This director is now implementing this practice, which breeds loyalty.

Approaching potential mentors

Be patient and build connections through regular interactions, evolving conversations in the office, over lunch or outside of the office. Don't wait for a potential mentor to invite you to lunch or coffee – you make the offer. Tell them you would love to hear about their background (people love to talk about themselves). Be direct in seeking their counsel in dealing with your own professional situations. Try to get on projects with them so you can demonstrate your personality and performance. If you do a good job with them, hopefully they will be impressed (and even see themselves in you). Bond over nonprofessional common interests. An African-American woman discovered a shared love of cooking with a senior white male executive, who often sought her out to exchange recipes.

You can try approaching speakers at seminars or classes; they may be receptive because they like working with younger, ambitious people who remind them of their younger selves and who are receptive to their wisdom.

Tips for Building a Relationship with a Potential Mentor

Kristi Anderson, executive recruiter, TMP Worldwide

Show overwhelming interest in their kids! Pretend you like their kids, remember their names and ask about them often. Remembering to ask who won that high school football game will go a million miles in endearing yourself to a potential mentor.

Ask your mentor for advice often, even when you don't need it. People, especially successful people, like to hear themselves talk and to demonstrate their wisdom. Don't ask dumb or simple questions with a definitive answer, but ask your mentor open-ended questions regarding his style and experience in handling a particular business situation. Then just sit back and feign interest in the long-winded response. Even when I don't need the advice, I will pose such a question to a mentor. It makes a mentor feel like he is bringing you along in your professional development.

Establish a broad group of mentors

Cultivate different mentors for different areas of your professional life. You should not expect one person to provide all of the counsel and guidance you need to get ahead. Pick and choose different people you admire for different reasons and use them as a resource in areas where they shine. Quality matters too – one or two superstar mentors may do you more good in the end than a dozen slackers. Company and independent organizations for women and minorities are a great way to expand your network of mentors.

Getting the most from a mentor

Once you have mentors, be open to their advice. Do not be defensive – they have nothing to gain in giving you this advice. Mentors will only value and continue your relationship if you're communicative and sincerely value their counsel. Make sure you report back to them on your successes and setbacks.

Visit Vault at **www.vault.com** for insider company profiles, expert advice, career message boards, expert resume reviews, the Vault Job Board and more.

VAULT CAREER LIBRARY   97

How to Get a Mentor

Mary Cranston, chair of law firm Pillsbury Winthrop LLP

Mary is the chairperson of one of the largest law firms in America. She has been practicing law since 1975, and has litigated over 300 class action cases in state and federal court, focusing on antitrust counseling and litigation, and securities litigation. She has been named to the *National Law Journal*'s list of the 100 Most Influential Lawyers in America, and *California Daily Journal*'s list of the 100 Most Influential Lawyers in California.

Her advice on how to get a mentor:

Be a good mentee. Approach individuals who have skills you want to acquire. If you just say, "Help me," they will be less likely to help. But if you say, "I had a great idea; can we work on it together?" your chances are much higher. Think about how you can contribute to the relationship, then you're more likely to get help from a mentor.

Networking and Schmoozing

Schmoozing gets you contacts, friends and acquaintances. This network will prove invaluable when you are competing for scarce resources. Spend 80 percent of your networking efforts inside and outside of your company courting the top 20 percent of the most influential people in your world.

Super schmoozing locales

Attend work-sponsored social gatherings. In-office showers, birthday parties, happy hours and holiday parties may seem like a pain in the neck when you are trying to get your work done. But in reality, they are an ideal time to meet and mingle with people from other departments and senior executives with whom you might not usually cross paths. Don't be shy. Walk up to people and introduce yourself. Make sure you know the names of senior executives you approach (ask your boss to point out who is who in the room). Keep it simple and friendly, for example, "Hi, John. We haven't had the chance to work together, but I'm Bill, marketing analyst. I work with Sally on the new product launches." Follow up with the new people you have met after the party is over. Either drop by their office to say hello, or invite them to lunch.

Use social events outside of the office as a chance to make important business connections. Attend parties hosted by successful or well-connected people, charitable benefits or cultural events (e.g., gallery opening, premiere party). One female attorney in Silicon Valley went to one party and got on the quarterly invite list to huge parties thrown by local venture capitalists. Be prepared at these gatherings to talk about yourself – what you've done and what you want; otherwise, people won't be able to help you achieve your goals. Even if your new contacts can't help you immediately, if you keep in touch with them, they may come across something or someone helpful to you in the future.

Join professional, cultural and alumni-based associations. Everyone has a natural network. Not only are there industry associations, ethnic or cultural associations, and alumni groups you can and should tap into, there may even be an organization that combines multiple dimensions of your demographic (e.g., Harvard Black Alumni club, Women in Digital Media association, Asian American Bar Association). Find and be active in these organizations. One lawyer spoke on a panel for women lawyers in intellectual property and got re-acquainted with an old classmate who placed her at her next job.

Who You Know Helps Your Career
Mae-Ling Tien, former Apple Asia developer programs manager

There's no doubt in my mind networking or "who you know" can make a significant impact on a person's career. My first job out of college was at Apple Computer. At the time, there was an internal organization called the Apple Asian Association (AAA) that I joined. Over the course of a couple of years, I became extremely involved with AAA, organizing conferences and building relationships with a group of colleagues from almost every department and various levels of management.

The networking with AAA paid off one day when I decided to pursue a job opportunity in Hong Kong with Apple Asia. The position I was applying for was a two-grade jump. Due to standard hiring policies, promotions beyond one grade level were rare. After my first interview with the hiring manager (over the phone), I sent out an e-mail to five AAA Advisory Board members to ask them for letters of reference. WITHIN 24 HOURS, all five of these directors and vice-presidents had drafted and e-mailed letters to the hiring manager in Hong Kong! The next time I

Visit Vault at **www.vault.com** for insider company profiles, expert advice, career message boards, expert resume reviews, the Vault Job Board and more.

VAULT CAREER LIBRARY   99

spoke to the hiring manager, his first comment was "You have a few friends."

I received the job offer without ever having a face-to-face meeting with the hiring manager. To this day, I attribute the opportunity to fulfill a life-long dream of working in Hong Kong to the relationships I built in AAA.

Other places to network. Do not limit networking to the workplace. You never know who someone knows, so be vocal about your professional goals. Your family can help you find contacts. You can also get contacts through your friends. Other sources include professors, classmates, career centers and alumni.

Use Lunch to Network

Mary Glasser, former PriceWaterhouseCoopers consultant and Ticketmaster executive

For a long time, I got into the bad habit of eating lunch at my desk. In reality, making lunch dates with people is a great way to get to know your colleagues, especially those who don't work in your department. Everyone has to eat at some point, and it is nice to get out of the office and into a casual environment to chat, even if the conversation is about work. Try to seek out people outside of your department for lunch dates, and try to have lunch with different people all the time, rather than just recycling the same few friends.

How to make a good impression

- **Be genuine.** People can tell if blatant self-interest or superficiality motivates your interaction with them.

- **Use direct eye contact and a firm handshake** when introducing yourself. You make the strongest impression in the first minute.

- **Find out what interests the other person,** whether it's work or nonwork related. Everyone loves to talk about himself!

- **Compliment something about the other person.** Whether it is about his shoes, her business suit, what you have heard about his management style or how well you have seen her present in front of a large group, everyone loves to be flattered when the sentiment is genuine.

- **Listen carefully and attentively.** Acknowledge what you have heard, for example by nodding or asking questions about something the other person said. If you're a good listener, people will want to talk to you.

How to cultivate your network

- Be organized in tracking and remembering people's names, jobs and some interest they have. When you get a business card, you can jot down some notes about the person. If possible, don't write on the card in front of the person. (In some Asian cultures, writing on business cards is deeply offensive!)

- Maintain some sort of regular contact with your contacts.

  - Drop someone a short e-mail or voice mail to say hello once in a while.

  - Send an annual Christmas card from your company.

  - Schedule occasional coffee, lunches or drinks. It cements a relationship to see someone in person from time to time. Organize a group activity to save yourself the time of seeing multiple people individually.

  - Congratulate people when you see them in the news.

- Be proactive in helping others. When it comes to networking, it's important to demonstrate that you're not just out for yourself. Sharing information is a great way to be helpful.

  - Send an article or event information of something that interests them.

  - Introduce two of your contacts who don't know each other but have something interesting in common.

  - If you are asked for help, help.

Visit Vault at **www.vault.com** for insider company profiles, expert advice, career message boards, expert resume reviews, the Vault Job Board and more.

VAULT CAREER LIBRARY   101

Fitting into Corporate America as a Minority

CHAPTER 10

The corporate world is still largely led by heterosexual white men. The culture of the workplace makes sense to them. However, if you are a woman, gay, a person of color or a foreign national (or any combination thereof) you may not automatically have had the same advantages, philosophies or perspectives. You may often be the only minority on the project team or in a meeting.

If you're not a straight white man, don't be discouraged. There is no barrier to your success, as long as you understand corporate culture and uphold the written and unwritten rules at an even higher standard. To succeed, it helps if you:

- Demonstrate undeniable ability.

- Make fewer mistakes.

- Understand that the rules may work a bit differently where you're concerned.

The Importance of Understanding Your Company's Culture
An African-American Wall Street analyst

Sometimes people, especially minorities, come from a background where they don't have all the resources. They really need to understand how things work to help avoid trouble, petty pitfalls and landmines that people can point to in an adversarial environment. If someone doesn't like you and it's not your fault, you can't give them anything to hold against you. You might not be able to make the mistakes others make.

Appearance

Take extra care in your appearance. It is the first impression you make in terms of your professional credibility, and it will be easy for others to be judgmental of your looks. As a new hire at the bottom of the food chain, you should not be making any personal statements with your clothes. Nothing should distract from the quality of your work. Strive to look well-groomed and polished, a look you can achieve on any budget.

Presentation Counts
Siobhan Green, project manager

At my performance evaluation for my first job, I was shocked to be rated poorly on my professional appearance. When I asked what that meant (I had a good wardrobe and thought I was more or less fitting in with the other staff), I was told that I should "dress more like Judy." So I watched her and noticed the difference. I didn't wear makeup and she did. Her hair, face and nails were always impeccable – and mine weren't.

The president of our company, whom I often accompanied to client meetings as a note taker, was the one who gave me the low review. He didn't really know what made Judy look more professional than me, but it bothered him enough to mention it to my supervisor and note it on my evaluation. I realized that if I wanted to continue working in that company, wearing nice suits would not be enough. I would have to make sure my nails were always clean and polished, get my hair trimmed regularly, and wear some eyeliner and lipstick, at least for meetings with clients and senior managers.

- **Dress appropriately for your industry and for your position.** Dressing outside your company norm suggests a lack of judgment and cultural fit.

- **Dress well to appear older.** Often, women and minorities can look much younger than their age. Remember that you will interact with senior executives and clients who are two to three times your age. One easy way to appear older, and more professionally credible, is to dress in a more subdued, conservative style. If you are wearing a suit, you are less likely to be mistaken for the summer intern or bike messenger.

- **Women should avoid inappropriately sexy clothes.** There is no quicker way to hurt your professional credibility. If you want to be taken seriously, observe limits: don't bare your midriff, wear low-cut necklines, see-through blouses or Ally McBeal-length miniskirts. Save it for the weekend (unless you are coming into the office). Use the 50 percent rule for judgment calls: if at least half the women go without pantyhose, wear open-toed shoes or moderately short skirts, then you can.

- **Minorities can display ethnic style - in moderation.** Wearing a kente-cloth pocket square with your suit is fine, but coming to work in a full-on dashiki is not. If you wear a piece of clothing for religious reasons (a yarmulke or a headscarf, for example), select pieces in subdued colors and make sure the rest of your clothing fits company standards.

- **Geeky isn't chic in the workplace.** Does your wardrobe consist of square glasses and faded T-shirts with funny slogans? Then you'll need to invest a little bit of time and money in upgrading your look. Overhauling your image will boost your self-esteem and the respect you command from others. Unfortunately, the bottom line is that co-workers in corporate America can be even more superficial than bullies in the schoolyard.

  - No clue what to wear? Buy some fashion magazines, ask your stylish colleagues some questions about where they shop, or talk to a sales clerk in the men's department in a classy department store or chain like Brooks Brothers.

  - Replace your glasses with simple wire frames.

  - If you work in a formal dress environment, aim to have three or four tailored suits, twice as many shirts and ties, two pairs of dress shoes (one brown and one black) and four casual outfits for Fridays. If you work in a business casual environment, aim to have at least four or five nice slacks (e.g., black, gray, khaki, navy blue, olive), twice as many shirts to mix and match and two pairs of casual shoes (one brown and one black). Women should buy simple suits in neutral colors (black, brown, gray). Your mint green pantsuit may look smashing on you, but it's so memorable that you won't be able to wear it more than once a month. A simple black skirt suit, on the other hand, can be worn at least once a week. In addition, you can split up the skirt and the jacket and wear them with other items to create more work-ready looks.

  - Remember that sock color needs to match shoe or pant color. And never wear athletic socks with a suit! Women, if you're wearing a skirt, wear non-shiny nude or black hose only.

Visit Vault at **www.vault.com** for insider company profiles, expert advice, career message boards, expert resume reviews, the Vault Job Board and more.

VAULT CAREER LIBRARY   **105**

Dressing Right Brings Respect
Former management consultant

When I started working, I brought with me all my clothes and shoes from college and summer jobs. I learned very quickly that while chunky heels and open-toed shoes, fitted tops and above-the-knee skirts weren't necessarily prohibited, I felt much better about myself and the respect I got from senior management by dressing more conservatively. And so my career wardrobe began with new French blue button-down shirts and conservative black pants.

• **Get your hair cut once a month** by someone other than your mother. Men, part your hair on the side instead of the middle.

• **In America, follow American standards.** Overseas, it can be quite common for corporate employees to wear the same outfit several times a week and not shower every day. Be forewarned that Americans who work in a corporate environment are typically extremely superficial about wardrobes and downright fanatical about personal hygiene. If you want to fit in as much as possible, shower and use deodorant every day, and try to have at least five fresh outfits in your wardrobe, one for every day of the week.

Communication

Women and minorites sometimes don't communicate as well as they could. Here are some tips to make sure you're heard and appreciated.

Be direct

Out of insecurity or lack of confidence, women and minorities often say things in passive-aggressive or indirect ways. They may lack confidence in their opinions or be afraid of hurting someone else's feelings. You waste everyone's time when you don't let your manager and your peers know what you need in order to succeed in your environment. Nobody can read your mind; it is up to you to take responsibility for your own work successes and failures.

Ask questions

Questions are your friends. If you don't understand something, ask for clarification. If you don't understand the explanation, ask again. If you are in a meeting and don't want to ask your questions in front of the whole group, write down your question and follow up with your manager or the appropriate party afterwards.

If you are not sure how to do an assignment, it is vital to ask questions until you feel confident about the tasks ahead of you. If you feel uncomfortable questioning your manager or if your manager is unavailable, ask peers to help you interpret the assignment or find out if co-workers have done a similar project in the past. After you get a better sense of what the project is about, return to the assigning manager with more focused questions. For example, you can say, "I just wanted to make sure I understand what you want – should the analysis address the issue of [XYZ] by evaluating these two assumptions?"

Manage your workload and your manager

You might think that the more work you do, the more you will be valued. You might be tempted to keep accepting assignments and duties, regardless of their relevance to your role. Stop! Be realistic about your ability to do high-quality work. Refuse work if you don't have time to do a thorough, thoughtful job. If you miss a deadline, your manager won't care that you had too much on your plate.

Do not expect your manager to know your limits. If you have too much "essential" work, approach your manager, let her know that you're already pushed to your limit and ask her to help you prioritize your assignments. That's your manager's job!

Contribute your thoughts to work conversations

Women and minorities are often intimidated by the prospect of speaking up in a meeting. Maybe you were told all your life not to challenge elders. Maybe you assume that if others talk firmly and confidently, they know what they're talking about. Maybe you are afraid of looking silly or less than perfect in any way.

Snap out of it! In the professional world, you will be judged on your ability to speak up and express yourself in a clear, thoughtful, articulate way. It

Visit Vault at **www.vault.com** for insider company profiles, expert advice, career message boards, expert resume reviews, the Vault Job Board and more.

VAULT CAREER LIBRARY   **107**

doesn't matter if what you say is "right" or "wrong." It's about participating in the dialogue as a confident, critical thinker. Emulate colleagues who are articulate, confident, proactive speakers. Notice how they express themselves: when they break into a conversation, how they phrase challenges in a nonthreatening way, how they respond to criticism of their ideas. Do not view speaking up as a "challenge" to your superiors, but rather a demonstration of your thoughtful consideration of a work issue.

Accept praise and criticism with grace

While humility is a good characteristic, women and minorities are particularly harsh judges of their own performance. Celebrate your successes. When your peers, managers and clients compliment you, accept the praise with a smile, a nod and a sincere "Thank you! I appreciate your generosity." If you can't handle the limelight, as soon as you accept the praise, deflect the attention by sharing credit with your team.

Often, people assume that everyone is just as talented as they are. Not true! Just because writing detailed, informative memos is easy for you doesn't mean that it's equally easy for all your peers. Don't underestimate yourself.

Learn from your failures, but don't dwell on them. Everyone makes mistakes, and you do yourself a disservice to dwell upon your missteps. Just because you made a mistake doesn't mean you aren't doing a fantastic job. Someone else in your position could have made twice as many mistakes. Don't take criticism as a personal attack. Just accept it as a lesson learned and don't make the same mistake next time.

Women and Emotions

Women and men are both emotional in their own ways, but the corporate world is much more attuned to, and accepting of, traditional male emotional response (arguing, back-slapping, yelling) than female emotional response (hugging, crying, self-deprecation). If you're a woman, try to cut back on classic female emotional responses. While it'll take some practice, it is necessary for you to detach emotions from your day-to-day work routine. You can still be very loyal to your company, friendly with your colleagues and accountable for your work without bringing your personal standards and sensitivities into the office.

Distinguishing between personal friendships and work relationships

Women often blur the lines between work friendships and personal friendships. While it is great to like your colleagues so much you want to be "real" friends with them, you need to respect appropriate professional boundaries at all times. In the office, your work relationship trumps your personal friendship. If you have or your colleague has access to confidential work information, you cannot expect to share that information as gossip. You and your colleague may have lunch or coffee every day, but that person may not necessarily want to socialize with you outside of the office. If one of you actually reports to the other, or you just work very closely together, understand that constructive criticism needs to be shared from time to time for professional growth; it's not a personal insult. If you and your colleague have a pre-existing friendship before you started working for the same company, don't slip into comfortable socializing patterns in front of others in the office. It will diminish your professional credibility if everyone thinks you spend all your time gossiping with each other instead of producing for the company.

Being the bitch

It's a well-known double standard – a man stands his ground, and he is called authoritative. A woman stands her ground, and she is called a bitch. A woman may be labeled "bitchy" for saying the same thing a man could say without repercussion. Anticipate these responses and move beyond them.

- Stay firm. Do not raise your voice. Never, ever whine.

- Always listen attentively to a different view and try to understand other perspectives. But it's perfectly appropriate to say "no" if you have good reasons to counter objections.

- Learn to present your views and arguments in a linear, logical fashion. Otherwise, your valid points will be lost, and you may even be considered "irrational."

- Manage your day and control factors that make you cranky. Try to avoid situations that you know will set you off. For example, if you can't stand a certain co-worker, try not to work with that person. If you can't stand a certain manager, try to present your findings to a more sympathetic listener. If you get cranky when you are tired, make sure you get enough sleep

Visit Vault at www.vault.com for insider company profiles, expert advice, career message boards, expert resume reviews, the Vault Job Board and more.

VAULT CAREER LIBRARY   109

before important meetings. If you get cranky when you are hungry, stock snacks in your office and eat them!

Crying in the office

It is not a shameful thing to cry in the office – it happens all the time! It is a reflection of how much you care about your job, and your strong feeling of accountability. Unfortunately, women are more susceptible to crying than men, and the corporate world does not know how to deal with a crying woman. If you feel yourself getting teary, excuse yourself, dry your tears and return to the meeting or conversation.

If you feel mortified that you lost control of your emotions in front of your male boss, take comfort. You are not the first person he has seen cry, and you will certainly not be the last. And if your boss is a longtime veteran of the business world, he has seen much crazier things than a woman crying in the office. If you start crying in front of a female boss, you can expect one of two responses. Either she will comfort you because she remembers all the times it happened to her in the past, or she will be frustrated that you are being too girly. If she takes the latter stance, it is probably because she is dealing with her own insecurities of being a woman in a man's world, and you shouldn't take it personally. Just move on.

If you cry once in a blue moon, your co-workers will shrug off your rare crying jag. If it happens often, however, people will begin to doubt your emotional stability (even if it's their fault that you are crying). For your own physical and emotional health, get out of an environment that regularly pushes you to tears.

Developing crushes on senior executives

The work environment is sometimes the first time that a young woman will build a close relationship with an older man who is not a relative. Sometimes, women look to their boss or mentor as a father figure. It is common for young women to develop crushes on senior executives. These crushes are often rooted in admiration for the senior executives' professional expertise and accomplishments. Conversely, the wide-eyed enthusiasm and sometimes blatant worship demonstrated by newbies can be quite flattering, even tempting, to the senior executives.

It's flattering to gain the attention of any senior executive. But even if your interactions are completely platonic and legitimate, keep an eye out for any hints of romantic impropriety. As tempting as it is to have a secret affair with someone older and more powerful, it is not worth the toll on your emotions and the possible consequences on your career. If you think there's a chance of some illegitimate romantic interest, change your behavior. Be polite, but do not discuss personal matters. Try to find other mentors. Above all, avoid being alone with the person, especially after business hours. Remember that even if your behavior is impeccable, if you start having long lunches with a superior, meeting him after work on a regular basis, etc., others will suspect that you're having an affair anyway. In such situations, the junior person almost inevitably loses out.

Dealing with Stereotyping

People stereotype others out of ignorance and convenience, not malice. As a minority in the corporate world, you may find yourself subtly or blatantly treated differently than your peers because of your assumed strengths, weaknesses and traits. This special treatment may not necessarily be unpleasant or negative. But you need to identify who is making what assumptions, and how these erroneous assumptions impact your work life. If there is any negative impact on your image at the company, and hence your long-term professional development, it is important to address the situation gracefully and request the same treatment your peers receive.

Stereotyping is often unconscious on the part of your colleagues. For example, there's an old stereotype that all Asians are good at math. And maybe you are Asian and really are quite good at math. So on, say, your first management consulting project, it seems to make sense for you to do the back office analysis while someone else interviews the client executives. But the more you do the back office number-crunching, the better you become at it, and the more it makes sense for you to do it again next time. Eventually, if you keep holing up with your calculator, you will fall behind in developing communication skills, professional presence and client relationships. Break the cycle and make sure you are learning an appropriately broad set of skills before you become pigeonholed as the "expert" of one task.

In the next section, we will outline common stereotypes of women, minorities and gay men. Specific ethnicities, age groups and sexual orientation will trigger specific stereotypes. These examples are meant to give you some idea of direct and indirect discrimination you may face based on commonly-held stereotypes. Generally, stereotypes stunt your professional development by skewing the mix of work you get, while your peers receive a more balanced training.

Visit Vault at **www.vault.com** for insider company profiles, expert advice, career message boards, expert resume reviews, the Vault Job Board and more.

V/\ULT CAREER LIBRARY   **111**

If you decide you are fine with the situation because it is an anomaly, is short-term or has upsides, that's fine. If you want to change the situation, you have to speak up early before the precedent is repeated too often. Whether or not you want to address the stereotype directly, at least you can inform your manager that you would like to broaden your skill set and get a good mix of challenging and diverse work. Don't approach your boss complaining. Tell him your reasoning and your proposed solutions, so that you steer the conversation toward getting his support for one option and the transition itself is assumed. The sooner you demonstrate consistent, undeniable interest and accomplishment in the areas outside of the stereotype, the sooner people will see you as a unique individual. It is not fair that it takes extra work, but the investment is worth it.

Common Stereotypes: Women

Assumption	Situation	Solution
You are bad at math but good at writing.	Whenever project tasks are distributed amongst the team, you always get the qualitative, not quantitative, tasks. You don't become better at math. If you are put on a quantitative task and have trouble with it, you are removed from the task instead of trained to do it better.	Make it a priority to learn new things, especially when you first start your job. Do not let yourself be removed from quantitative projects.
You are suited to detailed administrative work.	You are assigned administrative duties no one else wants: taking notes at the meetings, booking travel for the team, making copies, ordering lunch, getting coffee for clients, setting up or cleaning up a meeting.	Volunteer someone else for the task and try to get your manager's backing.
You are eye candy and probably not that bright, because you're attractive.	You are excluded from important meetings, but trotted out on fun business development outings so older male clients can flirt with you. People gossip about you.	Make sure your work stands on its own. Do not dress in a revealing or sexy manner.
You are too sensitive and emotional.	You don't get direct feedback about your performance so you don't advance. People are afraid you will cry, so they treat you gently. When you do cry, people assume you cannot handle stressful work.	Seek out truthful feedback. Remove yourself from stressful situations and control your temper and emotions.
You are timid.	People forget to ask you for your opinion because they assume you won't have one. You stop having opinions because you are never asked about them, stunting your critical thinking and communication skills.	Practice expressing yourself. Build alliances. Emulate strong speakers.
You are a pushover.	You are asked to do work that no one else wants to do, like staying late in the office for a last minute assignment, cleaning up other's unfinished work, and delivering bad news for other people.	Learn your boundaries. Embrace the word "No," especially if these requests do not come from a manager or senior executive.
You are a token hire.	Especially in a macho environment like investment banking or sales, your peers don't believe you made it here on merit, and do not give your work and opinions equal respect.	Work twice as hard to prove yourself. Try not to be too sensitive about routine male-bonding behaviors.
Work is not as important to you as it is to your male co-workers. Your family comes first.	Co-workers will not ask you for help on tough assignments. Your manager may be reluctant to invite you on business trips or to late-night client dinners.	Meet every deadline. Do not discuss family visits or shopping excursions, especially if you take time off for these activities. Clearly state your interest in attending a client event.

Visit Vault at www.vault.com for insider company profiles, expert advice, career message boards, expert resume reviews, the Vault Job Board and more.

VAULT CAREER LIBRARY   113

The de facto secretary

Women are often unconsciously slotted into an administrative role and given routine, detail-oriented work. While these projects may be important, and it's vital to be able to pitch in during a time crunch, it's difficult to shine by doing these routine tasks. The requests may seem benign at first. Can you take the notes during the meeting? Can you prepare FedEx packages? Can you coordinate the next meeting or the next business trip? If you are the most junior person on the team, assume that status is the reason for getting these chores. In the corporate world, the guy at the bottom of the food chain takes care of all the scrub work. The more machismo-laced an environment you work in, the more pronounced the hierarchy will probably be. Check with the second-most junior person to see if he had all the same "chores" before you arrived. Make sure you pass those duties on right away when a more junior person joins the team.

If you are not the most junior teammate, you may have been designated as a secretary for the team because of your gender. How should you handle the request? If the need is legitimate and you are the most appropriate person to perform the task (e.g., because you have the time or because your piece of the work is not as time-sensitive), go ahead and do it, and don't take it personally. If the need is not legitimate, or you are not the most appropriate person for the job, do not accept the role! Ask your manager to pass the chore to a secretary or another member of your department. Or tell your manager you would like to rotate the responsibility around the team because you took the duty last time. You could simply say, "I'm sorry. I don't have time to do that and meet my other deadlines. Can someone else pitch in?"

If a client asks you to do something administrative, go ahead and do it … once. Make sure you raise the issue with your manager and get his backing before you tell the client you cannot the second time. If you are asked to do something really demeaning, like making coffee, smile sweetly or make a little joke and say you don't know how to.

If you are the only woman on the team and you are constantly performing the admin duties, you will diminish your professional credibility and stunt your professional development compared to your male peers. Address the situation politely but directly with your manager and/or other perpetrators. Here are two common scenarios women in the corporate world face and how to address them.

Address and Retrain Your Manager Immediately If You Feel Singled Out

Sonja Beals Iribarren, former director at Disney

As the most junior member of the team, I accepted the fact that I drew the duty of making copies during meetings, should the need arise. That I was often the only woman in the room seemed only a coincidence until a new, younger – and male – analyst joined the team. I think we were both shocked when my boss again asked me to step out and make a few copies at the next meeting. I did so without complaint, in the name of team spirit, but did speak to my boss privately immediately afterward and told him that I wanted that duty to fall to the new junior member of the team. I tried to keep the focus on the seniority issue and away from any discussion about gender, which I felt might be interpreted as militant feminism and would not ultimately serve my purpose. I was concerned that people's perception of me would be negatively affected if I continued to accept this duty without comment. It's not about making the copies – it's that people expect you to stand up for yourself. Honestly, I wouldn't be surprised if scenarios like these aren't a test to see how you handle yourself in these situations.

The note-taker

You are always asked to take notes "because you have the best handwriting." This statement could be absolutely true – some guys really have atrocious handwriting!

But when you take notes, you are busy looking down at the paper and writing down what everyone else says. As a result, you don't get to participate in the discussion as much. At review time, your manager won't recall hearing you speak in meetings, forgetting that he asked you to take notes. He'll have the impression that you are timid (playing right into another common stereotype of women). Furthermore, if you are writing madly in a future meeting that includes a client or a senior executive, you lose the opportunity to interact with and impress an important person. You may even be mistaken for a secretary yourself.

If you are the most junior person on the team, you may have to take notes until someone new is hired. If you are not the most junior person, get a reality check from a trusted peer or manager in the office who is removed from the situation at hand. "I want to ask your opinion because I'm not sure if I am being too sensitive. Who takes notes in your meetings?"

Visit Vault at www.vault.com for insider company profiles, expert advice, career message boards, expert resume reviews, the Vault Job Board and more.

VAULT CAREER LIBRARY   115

The cyclical nature of stereotyping comes from the fact that the more you do something, the better you become at it than everyone else, so then everyone wants you to continue doing it. After several meetings of being the note-taker, you learn to outline exactly how your boss likes it, type everything up with graphs and charts inserted, and distribute to the group quickly. Of course everyone will want you to keep doing it because no one else does it as well. But continuing the role compromises your professional development, self-respect and the respect of your peers, even if it is gradual and unintentional.

Talk to your manager directly, but avoid any suggestion that the offense was intentional (even if you suspect it was). Address the professional rationale behind your request and your proposed solutions. "I don't want to always be the note taker because it prevents me from participating in the discussion in a meaningful way. The issues are so interesting I'd like to share my thoughts next time. Let's rotate the responsibility, or bring a secretary into the meeting to take the notes."

Be prepared to be brushed off as being hypersensitive. "Uh oh, you're not a militant feminist are you? You are way too sensitive!" Don't back down when faced with such resistance. Stand your ground, and calmly respond. "I know it's easy for you to jump to that conclusion, but humor me, and let's rotate the responsibility. I really would like to join in the conversation next time, and I think I have proposed fair solutions." Just make sure you don't clam up in the next meeting!

The teacher

Maybe you're repeatedly asked to train new hires. Why are you singled out every time? Is it because you are friendly, patient and verbal compared to your other colleagues? Is the responsibility of training only assigned to top performers who uphold the highest standards of work quality? Is training a total pain in the neck, and your boss knows you'll be a pushover? Ask your boss or the person who trained you how the responsibility is assigned. Then you can evaluate how you want to deal with the situation.

Perhaps you don't mind this assignment because you enjoy getting to know the new hires right away, you get a break from your normal workload and you get to expense more meals on the company. Or the training assignments reflect the fact that you're a star at the company. Maybe you actually hate sitting alone in your office all day crunching numbers and you really want to be a teacher at heart, so the opportunity to train new employees is a dream niche for you.

Now for the downsides. Because training is administrative, you may be expected to carry your full load of "real" work on top, meaning that you are working much later nights than everyone else to get everything done. Is training worth compromising your personal time? On the other hand, if your manager does reduce your workload to accommodate your training assignments, over time you might fall behind your colleagues in terms of advancement because you spend your days teaching and mentoring new hires instead of getting more challenging projects and interacting with senior colleagues and clients. Is training worth compromising your professional development?

Want to get out of doing training? Tell your boss you have already conducted the training twice as many times as the last person who did it. Or point out that you have missed client meetings because of training, which is detrimental to both your development and your relationship with your client. Suggest setting up a random system to rotate the responsibility amongst your peers by drawing numbers or assigning it alphabetically by last name. Or suggest that people pair up in teams to conduct training, so it's not as time-consuming for each person.

Common Stereotypes: Minorities

Assumption	Situation	Solution
You are good at math but bad at communicating.	You are always given back office analyses, but never put in front of senior executives or clients to present your findings.	Don't just hand over analyses to your manager with no explanation or interpretation. If you do a good job articulating your work to your boss, you can make the next step of presenting to others.
You have a chip on your shoulder.	People assume you are difficult to work with, keep their distance and minimize interaction. You leave the job without any significant relationships, mentors or networks to help you later on.	Be careful how you express your views. Show your casual, humorous side often.
You share the same traits as everyone else of your demographic.	You are compared to the other minority of the same race as you in the department. You are called the wrong name, as if people can't tell you apart. You compete with each other for the token slot.	Establish your identity and distinguish yourself.
You do not speak English well.	You are not given time to speak in meetings or written assignments.	Work to perfect your writing and speaking skills. Ask for and excel at, writing and speaking assignments.

Visit Vault at **www.vault.com** for insider company profiles, expert advice, career message boards, expert resume reviews, the Vault Job Board and more.

VAULT CAREER LIBRARY   117

People naturally categorize things into convenient buckets and make assumptions about those categories. Establish your own identity, and avoid "competing" with the one other person in the office of your race. For example, let's say that you are one of two Asian-American analysts in your starting class of twelve new hires. People you don't work closely with may mix you up and call you the wrong name. As a more serious pitfall, you may be compared to each other all the time, and there may also be an assumption that only one of you will be promoted.

Don't take it personally if the other person of your ethnicity is not quick to establish a close friendship with you. She may want to establish her own identity. It is an immature reaction on her part, but an explainable one. If a friendship is meant to be, over time it will develop as you both settle in to your new jobs.

Don't Assume You Will Bond Over Race
Former strategic planning analyst

During my interviews for a competitive position at a *Fortune* 100 company, I continually asked about the obvious lack of African-American employees in the department. To dispel my concerns, the recruiting manager arranged for me to meet a very senior African-American officer in the company, even though I would not actually be working with him in my prospective job.

Without thinking twice, I openly asked him about the dearth of African-Americans at the company. He replied, "If you are one of those black people who needs to be around other black people, you won't find them here!"

Shocked and disappointed, I quickly learned that not all people of color view themselves as leaders or mentors of junior employees of their same race. On the contrary, many prefer to ignore ethnicity and maintain distance from other colleagues of color in order to avoid labeling.

Ways of establishing your personal identity include:

- Socialize with a variety of your peers.

- Befriend the perpetrators. People will not mistake you for someone else if they get to know you. Talk about things you have in common. Let them get to know you as a person with distinct interests, rather than a token minority.

- Correct people if they call you by another name. You can do this nicely, but don't let them persist in thinking you are someone else. Correct the person on the spot, introduce yourself and laugh it off to help the perpetrator save face. "It's a big office, so I often forget names of people I've only met once or twice, too."

- Establish natural friendships with peers of your ethnicity. There is no advantage to discriminating against people who look like you, and you come off like a jerk. And you might be sacrificing a friendship with someone with whom you would otherwise really connect because of shared experiences and insights.

Geography Matters
Victor Hwang, former corporate lawyer, current COO LARTA (a nonprofit think tank)

If you're a minority, geography matters. I love Austin, Texas. I spent my formative years there. I love country music, barbecue, Longhorn football and big hair. I never encountered any overt prejudice in my professional life in Austin, but one does start to feel worn down after the third time someone has confused you with your minority co-worker, every lunch at a sushi restaurant starts a talk about "other Chinese food," and people think that your parents are Thai because they're from Taiwan. It may or may not be prejudice, really it's just ignorance, but it does take a toll on your self-esteem.

So I moved to Los Angeles and never looked back. There has been such a difference in my sense of professional opportunity since I've moved to Los Angeles. Climbing the professional ladder is hard enough already; one should eliminate as many controllable obstacles as possible.

Visit Vault at **www.vault.com** for insider company profiles, expert advice, career message boards, expert resume reviews, the Vault Job Board and more.

VAULT CAREER LIBRARY   **119**

Common Stereotypes: Gay Men

Assumption	Situation	Solution
You are creative.	People come to you with more questions and projects that involve visual aesthetic, creative design, or marketing, whether or not that is part of your job function.	Make it a point to shine in other areas. Make sure those areas are visible to management.
You don't have traditional masculine interests.	You are not invited to sports or bar outings. You miss out on the opportunity to network and bond out of the office.	Bring up your participation in sports, your home teams or your favorite non-gay bars and clubs. Invite yourself along.
You are checking out all the straight men in the office at all times.	Guys keep their distance. You are made to feel self-conscious.	Don't make any sexual references or jokes. Never flirt with or date co-workers.
You are flamboyant.	You are not put in front of the most conservative, stodgiest clients or senior executives.	Be mindful of corporate culture, behave conservatively and give people time to know you.
You are the token gay friend everyone wants.	Female colleagues want to be your best friend, talk to you about boys and fashion. Colleagues don't respect the same professional vs. personal boundaries with you. You're called "Will" from the popular show *Will and Grace*.	Be mindful of your interactions with others. Act professionally and conservatively, focus on work. Give people time to get to know the real you.

Do not hide your sexuality, but do not flaunt it either. Straight men are more likely to display prejudice when a gay man openly talks about sex and dating. Be discreet about your sex life, but feel free to treat your significant other by the same standards expected of straight colleagues. Bring your significant other as your date to company events, but refrain from public displays of affection (take note: the same goes for heterosexual couples). The bottom line is that there is no need to hide anything.

The Extra Importance of Building Relationships

Mentors

Decision-makers often consciously or unconsciously bond with and champion those who remind them of themselves. Minorities in particular need in-house mentors who champion them because they usually don't have natural role models and networks at their company. Mentors will educate you about your company's office politics and cultural norms, teach you valuable job skills and pass on industry knowledge.

You mentor does not need to share your minority status. In fact, a straight white male mentor can be a major asset in your rise up the corporate ladder. It takes time, patience and investment to develop a meaningful relationship with someone who seems to be very different from yourself – but it is worth it.

Finding a Mentor during a Meltdown
Ashley Fieglein, director, General Atlantic Partners

During my investment banking career, I learned the importance of choosing a mentor even though I was the only woman in an all-male office. Four years into investment banking, with hundreds of hours of lost sleep under my belt, I reached a moment where I really needed to let go. A client had yelled at me. I had a stack of work on my desk guaranteeing another lost weekend. And I had gotten a call saying that two of the projects were "urgent" and needed yesterday. I felt panicked. I noticed the teardrops on my desk, even though I wasn't aware I was crying. I got up and closed the door to my office. And the hysteria set in. I sobbed. And then I suddenly realized that I really wasn't going to be OK.

I picked up the phone and called one of the senior bankers with whom I had worked very closely over the four years. He showed up in my office in a matter of minutes. In spite of my embarrassment, I let him rub my back while I sobbed. He closed the door, gave me a glass of water and waited until I caught my breath.

He offered to help manage the situation, to get me more support and to get me more time. And then he sent me home. No arguments allowed, though I protested that things had to get done, but he insisted that they

Visit Vault at **www.vault.com** for insider company profiles, expert advice, career message boards, expert resume reviews, the Vault Job Board and more.

VAULT CAREER LIBRARY

121

would be OK I think he probably stayed extra hours that night to oversee the analysts working on my projects. I was sound asleep in my bed, catching up on some long overdue rest.

When I came back in the next morning, everything seemed manageable. The client who had reamed me the night before had called back to apologize. The work was no longer insurmountable. And the urgency had subsided.

My newly-found mentor never said a word to me about the incident afterwards. I ended up calling him crying at least once or twice more, and he always supported me kindly. He always took my tears seriously. He understood that this was my way of expressing anger. And I completely trusted his support of me.

Networking

Women and minorities should actively participate in professional associations to get to know successful peers and to learn from others who are in similar positions as you. But be careful to also seek out opportunities to connect with people outside of your demographic; otherwise, you risk limiting yourself. People are quick to feel threatened by what they don't understand, and you don't want to be stereotyped as narrow-minded or militant.

Eric Keene, a former McKinsey consultant who is African-American, advises, "Minorities and women should make special effort to attend the formal and not-so-formal social functions of the company. A lot of business/politicking gets done at these events, and a no-show can have greater consequences beyond not making face time with the partners."

The old boys' club

Accept the basic fact that the corporate world is not diverse – yet. Your exclusion from the old boys' network may span the benign (e.g., happy hour gathering) to the extreme (e.g., strip club outings, private golf courses). It's OK not to care whether you gain entrance into this community if you are happy to live without it. If you do care, there are varying approaches you can employ to gain acceptance over time:

- **Befriend a few key members, or get to know as many members as possible.** If you become friends with one or two ringleaders, you can get pulled into the circle. If everyone in the group knows who you are and has a generic but positive reaction to your name ("Hey, I know John too! He seems nice enough."), you may also get pulled into the circle. Try to identify one common interest you can bond over with each person, such as a common alma mater, favorite movie genre or sports team.

- **If you are a woman, it's OK to act like one of the guys, or to show your feminine side.** Lots of professional women go either way. For example, Ellen Hancock, former CEO of Exodus Communications, was known to hang out with her gang of male senior managers. Sherry Lansing, CEO of Paramount Pictures, is known for her soft management style. The most important thing is that you are comfortable in your actions, and that you interact with every person. If you really want to secure your place in the club, do not date anyone in the circle.

- **Develop some interests that overlap** with the group's common activities so that you can't be excluded due to your lack of ability, e.g., playing golf or tennis, or wine-tasting. It doesn't matter if you are mediocre at it; just get out there and participate. If you are really bad, take some lessons first.

- **Play up the fun and funny side** of your personality. These are the best traits to contribute to any group conversation or outing.

- **Evolve friendships naturally.** Employing the above strategies takes time. Do not barge your way into too many conversations or gatherings. It looks desperate. Invite a couple of co-workers to lunch or to drinks; they will likely reciprocate.

- **Make it easy to pronounce your name.** Don't take it personally if you have a name that people have a hard time pronouncing. Think of a good way to help people remember your name and feel comfortable addressing you. You can go by your initials, use the first syllable or two of your name as a nickname, or tell people what your name rhymes with when they first meet you. For example, Sucharita might tell clients who can't pronounce her name to call her "Su," or humorously spark their memory by telling them, "Just think of drinking a Margarita before you say my name."

Visit Vault at **www.vault.com** for insider company profiles, expert advice, career message boards, expert resume reviews, the Vault Job Board and more.

VAULT CAREER LIBRARY   **123**

Keep Your Private Life Private

If you work in a homogeneous environment, you may be subjected to greater scrutiny for being different, even in areas that are irrelevant to your work performance. If you suspect your colleagues are judgmental of your personal life, maintain distance between life inside and outside the office until you have earned your stripes as a respected member of the team or have a better read on the people you work with. No one needs to know about your sexual orientation, religion, extra-curricular activities, health situation or dating life.

Keep personal commitments on your calendar to yourself

The way you choose to spend your free time outside of the office may differ from your colleagues if you work in a homogeneous environment. Sometimes people will react with curiosity to those differences, and other times they will react with ignorance and insensitivity. Or even worse, your boss may pass judgment on whether your plans are important enough to approve your vacation request.

Some people are narrow-minded about gender-specific or culturally-based events on your calendar. Your co-workers may openly talk about or even plan buddy trips, bachelor parties, or Christmas, in front of you. But they can still make insensitive or ignorant remarks when you are trying to plan weddings, gay commitment ceremonies, bridal showers, baby showers, bachelorette parties or cultural, ethnic and religious events (e.g., "It's so unfair that you get extra days off just because you are Jewish!")

You may also experience discrimination for being single in the workplace. Your personal time may be considered less important than that of married co-workers because you don't have a family waiting at home for you. You may find that you are expected to work late or come in on weekends while your married teammates go home.

If you want to take time off without getting grief from your manager or your peers, protect your privacy around these events without sacrificing your values.

- Ask for time off based on a "family obligation" or "personal matter." There is no need to go into more detail.

- When planning events, use your office phone or Internet connection to make plans before or after your co-workers arrive at work, or during the lunch hour when fewer people are in the office. Or step into a conference room or an unused office to make a phone call.

- When planning events, take half a day off to run your errands or make your phone calls from home, rather than drawing attention to your upcoming event by coming and going from the office or making calls from the office.

- Avoid focus on female health concerns. Just tell your manager you are sick or have a doctor's appointment and leave it at that.

Don't talk about sex

Nothing diminishes your professional credibility more quickly than sexualizing yourself in the eyes of your colleagues. Just take a look at the endless headlines about political sex scandals. Even if the incident has nothing to do with the perpetrator's job, the perception is that one reflects on the other.

Women and gay men are treated with a double standard in this area. Be honest about your sexual orientation and your status with a significant other, but don't reveal details of your sex life to co-workers. They'll never look at you the same way again. And don't believe them when they say they'll keep something secret. You don't want to be the subject of office gossip.

Don't date co-workers

Unless you meet your soulmate, no good can come from dating in the office. A successful or a failed relationship can equally color your own and fellow co-workers' perceptions of twists and turns in your career path, regardless of how irrelevant the relationship is. The small probability of meeting your soulmate and living happily ever after is not worth the much greater probability of having to work with an ex after a bad breakup.

If you are going to do it anyway, keep it discreet. Make sure you have earned respect as a valuable team member before making the relationship public knowledge. Even after you are public, always maintain a high level of discretion. It's like a tree falling in the forest when no one is around – if you break up and no one knows you were dating, you will be much better off. On the other hand, if you two get engaged and/or come out of the closet, most everyone will be happy for you.

Visit Vault at www.vault.com for insider company profiles, expert advice, career message boards, expert resume reviews, the Vault Job Board and more.

VAULT CAREER LIBRARY   125

Sexual Harassment

Sexual harassment is truly the dirty little secret of Corporate America. **The important things to remember if you are a victim of sexual harassment are that you are not alone, and it is not your fault.** If you get a group of women in a room, each one will be able to contribute a story about herself or a friend dealing with unwelcome and inappropriate advances from a peer, a manager, a senior executive or a client. Women don't talk about these experiences openly for a number of reasons. They can't believe it happened to them. They wonder if they were at fault. They don't want to damage their professional credibility.

Different variables may affect your exact approach to dealing with a harasser. How offended are you? Is it a one-time offense that you can ignore, or is it a recurring issue that will worsen if you don't address it? Keep in mind that you probably won't be the first or last person harassed by this perpetrator. Maybe he doesn't even know he is harassing you and the situation requires a polite but frank confrontation. Give the harasser the benefit of the doubt if the offense is more irritating than threatening. "You probably don't realize it, but you are making me really uncomfortable, and I don't want to feel that way around you because I think you are a great guy and we work so well together." "I am flattered that you are attracted to me, but I am not interested in extending our relationship beyond our professional interaction."

Who is the perpetrator? Is it a peer or the goofball in the mailroom who you can directly confront with confidence? If you want to escape a sticky situation with an important senior person without causing a scene, humor and white lies are the best weapons. Let's say a senior executive has you cornered at an office party, and you don't want to get on his bad side with a rude exit. Tell him you need to go to the bathroom and don't return. Surround yourself with safe peers or superiors so that he can't corner you again. If he asks you why you didn't return, innocently tell him you ran into another colleague in the bathroom and got sidetracked in a conversation.

Whom do you tell? If you can't laugh off the situation, talk to someone you trust to get another perspective. That person doesn't need to be your manager. Try to decide whether your manager will be your ally in dealing with the situation. This likelihood has nothing to do with your manager's gender. A woman could act conserned or act annoyed that you are making a mountain out of a molehill, because she has dealt with harassment her whole career. A man could either downplay the "flattery," or immediately see the situation for what it is and take it seriously. If you have no idea how to handle the situation and no obvious confidante to tell, a good first step is talking to your own manager or the human resources manager.

Unwelcome Client Advances
Former Wall Street analyst, an African-American woman

I was attending a financial conference with my investment banking team and meeting many prospective clients. One executive seemed particularly attentive and I was excited by the prospect of bringing business into the company and being a hero. When the executive suggested we meet up for dinner after the conference for further discussions, I agreed and told him which hotel I was staying in.

Later that afternoon, the executive called me to make plans to meet for dinner. I asked if he had spoken to my manager to include her. He said "no" in a way that implied he had no intention of including her. I immediately realized I was not comfortable with the situation. The possibility of bringing business to my company was not worth the risk of being naïve about the man's interests. I politely told him I had changed my mind and could not join him for dinner. He told me that he understood my reservations, an awkward answer that only confirmed my intuition.

After much thought, I decided to mention the incident to my manager. I was hesitant because I did not know if she would think I botched up establishing a new client relationship. My manager was the only female managing director in my division. I knew how important it was for her to continually build her client base. However, I wanted my manager to hear it directly from me first, in case the potential client mentioned the incident to her later. I also hoped in some way that she would make me feel better about what had happened, perhaps sharing similar situations that she had confronted in her many years in the business.

The next day I confided in my manager, who was not sympathetic at all and accused me of overreacting. She acted angry that I even told her about the event. I was incredibly hurt and disappointed that she didn't treat my anxiety with more concern, if for no other reason than I was obviously upset by it. Though I always had a sense that she was threatened by me as the new and younger woman in the group, in this case I had expected her to show empathy and that we would bond over shared experiences. Instead I left her office feeling confused and judged.

Visit Vault at www.vault.com for insider company profiles, expert advice, career message boards, expert resume reviews, the Vault Job Board and more.

VAULT CAREER LIBRARY   127

Be Savvy in Declining Unwanted Advances

Marketing executive

While at a sales party, I was dancing with the head of the sales department and casually talking with him throughout the dance. At one point, he mentioned that it was fun and that we should go out sometime. Thinking that there was no way he could be serious, he was twice my age and married, I jokingly said that I wished he had a son for me to date. We both laughed and continued dancing and chatting.

Over a year later, after deciding to leave the company, I was conducting my exit interview with human resources. They informed me that I had been on probation for the last year and my performance had been under scrutiny. I was flabbergasted. I learned that the jilted colleague had filed a complaint that I was difficult to work with.

The Legal Lowdown

I feel like I've been discriminated against at work – what can I do?

If you feel that you are the victim of illegal discrimination at work, you must address it. Don't turn a blind eye and be a victim of actual discrimination. Make your voice heard and get the matter resolved.

Legally speaking, discrimination means unfair treatment of people. The most common types of discrimination that occur in the workplace are discrimination based on sex, race and age. Other types include family, marital and pregnancy status, national origin and physical and mental disabilities.

Harassment, sexual or not, is a form of discrimination. It is conduct that is unwelcome and intimidating, abusive or offensive. Sexual harassment falls into two categories: quid pro quo and hostile environment. Quid pro quo is basically "sleep with me or you're fired." Hiring, promotions and retention, for example, are influenced by whether or not an employee succumbs to requests for sexual favors. Hostile environment is unwelcome conduct that is severe enough to create an abusive work environment, for example derogatory comments or dirty jokes, offensive posters and pictures.

The harasser can be a supervisor or any other employee, regardless of position, or a non-employee such as an agent or contractor of the employer. To determine if the environment is hostile you must look at all the circumstances, such as the frequency and severity of the conduct (however, ONE act can constitute illegal harassment, depending on the circumstances) and whether your work performance is hindered. An employer can address issues of harassment in different ways, depending on the severity – from counseling and separating those who are involved to termination of the harasser.

If you feel you have been the victim of real discrimination, take action. First, unless you have concerns for your safety, directly tell the offender that the conduct is unwelcome and must stop. Then follow your company's specific grievance system. Employers must have policies against workplace discrimination that are well publicized, and effective means for implementing those policies, including clear steps that employees can follow to report the conduct and how an investigation will be carried out. If you feel the current system of your employer is not effective, tell someone you trust within the organization and get the ball rolling for change.

You should not tolerate discriminatory acts against you – your employer has a responsibility to prevent and eliminate any discrimination. But be prepared to look for a new job if your company's response is not acceptable. Some companies, even faced with the bald truth of discrimination, cannot, or will not, execute an acceptable resolution in a quick enough time frame.

Resources

For more information about managing gender-based interactions, check out Deborah Tannen's *Talking From 9 to 5 (Women and Men in the Workplace: Language, Sex, and Power)*. She is a professor of Linguistics at Georgetown University, and identifies all sorts of important and interesting communication differences and opportunities for misunderstanding between women and men in the workplace including conversational rituals, indirectness, the glass ceiling, women in positions of authority, sex and talking at meetings.

For more information about successfully climbing the corporate ladder beyond your first job as a minority, read David Thomas and John Gabarro's *Breaking Through: The Making of Minority Executives in Corporate America.* The authors are Harvard professors who have studied successful minority executives and compiled their advice for managing your career and making your mark in Corporate America.

Visit Vault at **www.vault.com** for insider company profiles, expert advice, career message boards, expert resume reviews, the Vault Job Board and more.

VAULT CAREER LIBRARY   **129**

Troubleshooting Common Problems

CHAPTER 11

Dealing With Mistakes

You will make mistakes. Accept that fact. What you can control are reducing your probability of making an error, quickly repairing any mistakes you do make, and creating a good relationship with your superiors and co-workers so they'll forgive your inevitable slipups.

Reduce the probability of making an error

- Check the logic of your piece of work in relation to the big picture. Does your piece fit into the story of the rest of the project?

- Triple-check the details. If, for example, you are working on a report, look for inconsistencies in specific numbers or general content between charts, tables, captions and text, your piece and the rest of the report, and the latest version of the document versus the last version. If you see something you don't understand, don't just chalk it up to your inexperience. You may have found a mistake.

- If you're doing an analysis, see if a peer can follow it. If she can't, it's probably too complex or set up incorrectly. Most business analyses are not that complex.

- If you are directed to do something you feel is wrong, keep a log of what you've been asked to do and what you've done to mitigate the situation, and triple-check your actions with your manager and your team.

Proofreading is Essential
Former management consultant

Reread everything. Twice. Then reread it again. No amount of proofing and checking is too much – the smallest mistakes can undermine long hours of hard work. Don't allow your credibility to be called into question because of carelessness!

If you make a mistake

- **Understand the impact** of the mistake. The biggest impact will be if a client sees your error. Let's say you discover a mistake in a calculation in a document you've produced. Is there a way to fix it quickly without calling more attention to it? Does it only affect one discrete area of your work, or is it referenced and used repeatedly in different sections? Is the math slightly off, or very off? Is it in the primary body of the work, or in back-up analysis in an appendix? The worst thing that you can do is scramble to address a mistake without realizing until later that the same mistake is repeated throughout a document.

- **Acknowledge the mistake** and the magnitude of its impact to your manager as soon as you discover it.

- **Immediately propose solutions** to fix the problem. Then fix it!

Solving the Problem

One late night in the office, minutes after a courier picked up several copies of the final client report to be delivered to different locations, Patty discovered a mistake in an analysis on one of the pages. Fearing the wrath of her meticulous project partner, but knowing it was less painful to confront and fix the problem now rather than let it come out in the upcoming client meeting, she marched into the partner's office and said, "In reviewing the report again, I discovered I made a mistake in the analysis summarized on page 12. The bottom line is off by less than $5,000, and the error only appears on that one page. Would you prefer for me to fax the client replacement pages or resend full reports with the correct page first thing in the morning? Either way, I'll leave messages for all package recipients tonight so they know the corrected version is forthcoming." Although the partner was not pleased about the mistake, there was nothing much to say in response other than her preferred fix. Patty immediately left the office to start faxing the replacement pages, so neither she nor her manager could dwell on the error.

- **Do not spend a lot of time explaining** why you made the mistake – you don't want your boss to dwell on the fact a mistake was made.

Moving on after Making a Mistake
Sonja Beals Iribarren, former director at Disney

One day, when I was groveling to the CFO again over some little stupid meaningless mistake I had made, he stopped short and said, "You never played organized sports, did you?"

I confirmed that I had not, wondering what this question had to do with anything.

He said, "You know how I can tell? Kids who play organized sports learn that you make a mistake, you shake it off and you get on with it. You over-apologize."

I changed my behavior overnight and, more importantly, watched how others react when confronted with a mistake. I believe that people will brush off your mistakes if you do, but will dwell on them if you grovel all day about them.

- When the problem has been resolved, try to identify the factors that contributed to the mistake (without assigning blame to specific people). Failures provide valuable lessons on how to prepare better and improve your performance. Don't assume the breakdown was an anomaly and doesn't need to be addressed. The discipline of reviewing mistakes is not nearly as uncomfortable as the humiliation of making the same mistake twice.

Your manager's response

Your manager has the power either to protect you or hang you out to dry when things go awry. Your manager will choose to protect you if you have developed a positive working relationship together and you have a great track record of high quality work.

Visit Vault at **www.vault.com** for insider company profiles, expert advice, career message boards, expert resume reviews, the Vault Job Board and more.

VAULT CAREER LIBRARY   133

No Support from Her Project Manager
Janelle McGlothlin, former market analyst

In my first job, I was a market analyst for a start-up company in consumer electronics. In that role, my primary job function was market research, but as in all start-ups, everybody pitches in where they need to. We were getting ready to launch a new, lower-cost version of the product and my boss (VP of marketing) asked me if I would take on some of the product management duties for the launch. Of course, I agreed. I was working on a team that was headed up by the director of marketing and the director of engineering.

As part of the new product rollout we were developing smaller packaging for the smaller product. I was given the task of calculating how many units fit on a pallet for the store displays, whether in the aisles or on an end-cap.

I miscalculated (forgetting that in addition to being thinner and not as wide, the box was also shorter). Unfortunately, this information had already been signed off on, and communicated to the retailers. We were going to end up with displays that came up to people's waists. Not a good merchandising tactic.

The VP called me into the director of marketing's office to ask what happened. I had no idea of the gaffe until that moment. As I explained the calculation, I realized I left out the height, so I told her that's where the screw up happened. As soon as I finished, the director of marketing said, "I thought there was a mistake in that when I reviewed it. Why didn't you catch that?" I was so shocked that as the team leader she didn't even try to take any responsibility for it.

Luckily, my boss was very cool and focused on solving the problem rather than reprimanding me. We ended up with a cardboard booster insert for the bottom of the pallet. As it turns out, we would have needed it anyway because the number of units on the pallet needed to make it a normal height would have been too large for most of the stores to handle. Needless to say, I watched my back with that director from then on.

Dealing with Work

I have way too much work!

If you juggle multiple projects and work with many different people, chances are your main manager doesn't know what's on your plate. If you are overloaded, it is your responsibility to speak up before there is a crisis. Be clear that your interest in decreasing your workload is to ensure top quality and timely work products, letting nothing falls through the cracks. Schedule a meeting with your manager, and:

• Provide your manager with a schedule of your projects, timelines and estimated time spent for each. Present the information in the format and medium that best works for your manager.

• Propose your own suggested prioritization. Ask your manager if he agrees, or how he would adjust the order of your assignments.

• Suggest solutions to manage your workload. For example, ask if you can give a project to someone else (check that person's availability first!), eliminate a redundant project or extend timelines.

• When you are working for different managers on different projects, often they won't be aware of each other's timelines. It is up to you to speak up when projects' deadlines are on crash courses, otherwise you will be blamed for not delivering. Once you have spoken up, it is up to your managers to specify how you should prioritize the work.

• Consider the possibility that you may indeed have to work harder. Many companies today don't offer a 9-to-5 work schedule. Assess your time commitment compared to your peers before approaching your manager.

How do I get a good mix of projects?

It is up to you to make sure you are getting a good mix of project types for the benefit of your own well-rounded education. Your managers don't have any real incentive to provide you with a broad array of projects. They will be tempted to keep giving you the same types of projects as you become better and faster at them. Furthermore, managers often specialize in certain projects themselves, so if they enjoy working with you and want to work with you again, you will start to specialize in the same kinds of projects. Insist on working on a broad array of projects in your first couple of years.

Visit Vault at www.vault.com for insider company profiles, expert advice, career message boards, expert resume reviews, the Vault Job Board and more.

VAULT CAREER LIBRARY   135

What happens if I sleep through a meeting?

If no one saw you, just get notes from a friend and, make sure you weren't assigned anything. Was it an important meeting? If so, and your boss seems displeased, you may want to pull your boss aside, quietly apologize, explain it was due to your long hours of hard work, and promise it will never happen again. If not, and your managers don't raise it with you (and don't seem angry in any way), you may just want to let it go, and make sure it doesn't happen again.

It is normal to be sleepy after a heavy meal, so plan ahead if you know there will be an afternoon meeting. Eat something light for lunch. During the meeting, drink cold water or something caffeinated, get up and go to the bathroom or stand behind your chair or against the wall for a few minutes to stretch your legs.

Interpersonal Problems

Bad managers

In the short term, there are survival strategies you can employ to deal with bad managers. In the long term, you need to get out. Here are some short-term fixes to common problems with your manager:

What if my boss hates me?

First of all, don't take things personally. It is unlikely that you alone are the source of your boss' anger. Try to figure out why the boss hates you. Is it valid? Is it just you, or everyone your boss manages? If your boss is mean to everyone, you'll be better able to cope with his animus. The most likely explanation, however, is that you are overreacting. Another possibility is that you are doing something wrong and your boss, instead of pointing out your error, behaves towards you in an exasperated or nasty manner.

Do Not Let Stress at Work Damage Your Health

Sue Schroeder, former senior financial analyst, First Interstate Bank

My first job after business school was in the prestigious Internal Consulting Group within the finance division of a large regional commercial bank. The department was filled with MBAs and PhDs, and I was the only woman in the group. Even the administrative assistant was a guy. It was the first place that I really experienced discrimination.

The problem was the person who hired me had left by the time I started work. In the meantime, my new boss was hired to join the group. When I showed up for work, he didn't like me on sight. I pride myself on being an affable person, and I had never encountered anything like this before. I tried to compensate by putting in longer hours than the rest of the guys in the group. It was such a good job that I pushed myself to tough it out and make it work. But I learned the hard way that some people won't like you no matter how hard you work or how smart you are. My success or failure in that position was outside of my control, but at the whim of my manager. It became such a stressful environment for me that I ended up with a stomach ulcer.

Luckily, I had established relationships with other people in the finance division. The CFO asked me to transfer to another job, which was the best thing that could have happened. I was able to start fresh in a new role and quickly advanced into larger roles within the bank.

The moral of the story is that life is too short to be in an unpleasant environment, especially if it endangers your health. There are always other opportunities out there, even if you don't see them at first glance. You have to learn to seek them out and that comes through networking and establishing relationships with co-workers, classmates, etc. Do not tolerate discrimination of any kind.

Talk to a mentor or trusted associate at the company about your boss. Disclose that you've been sensing that your boss doesn't seem to like you very much. If your mentor tells you that he's heard nothing of the sort, or if you learn that your boss simply has a somewhat unfriendly work style, then don't dwell on the issue. Do your best to relate to your boss in a friendly manner, especially at company events.

Visit Vault at **www.vault.com** for insider company profiles, expert advice, career message boards, expert resume reviews, the Vault Job Board and more.

VAULT CAREER LIBRARY   137

If your manager is truly abusive, evaluate your options:

- Can you change managers? If so, do it.

- Are you doing something that triggers the abuse?

- Have you talked to your boss? Let your boss know that you are not happy about his behavior. If your boss yells at you about a timeline, for example, you might say something like: "I understand your interest in completing this project on time, and there is no need to raise your voice while we are discussing the timeline." It is easy for your manager to continue the abuse if you silently accept it.

- Develop alliances, e.g., become very friendly with your manager's boss.

- If all else fails, do your best to get good training and develop relationships with other co-workers, and start looking for another job.

Dealing with a Problem Manager
Anonymous reporter

I was working as a reporter at a major metropolitan newspaper, and my relationship with my editor had turned sour. Initially, we had been pretty friendly, but for a variety of reasons (many of them related to her insecurity in her own position) she had turned against me. I think she was trying to puff herself up by making me look bad, which in turn would make her efforts seem more heroic.

I first tried talking with her directly about why she was suddenly unhappy with my work, why she had turned so unsupportive, and why I had heard her bad-mouthing me behind my back. (She was trying to convince the editor of my section – her direct boss – to demote me by sending me to a bureau.) She had nothing specific to say and ended up denying that anything was even wrong.

When the situation didn't improve, I decided I had to talk to the editor of our section. Luckily, I had a very good relationship with him, since he had hired me a few years before. He confirmed for me that my boss had indeed been trying to have me demoted, but told me not to worry because he had no intention of doing anything of the sort and thought I was doing a great job. I tried to explain that I still had a problem because my editor, who was supposed to be my advocate, had become so adversarial. All the section editor would say is, "You're both grown-ups; try to work it out." In general this would be fine advice, but when one of the parties in a conflict absolutely refuses to act like an adult, there's very little the other, well-meaning party can do.

I tried to take the high road for another week or so, but things kept getting worse. She was ripping up my stories and loudly complaining to other editors that she had to do so much work to make my copy suitable for the paper. I don't think the other editors really believed her, but it was still hard to ignore. I went back to the section editor again and he said he would talk to my editor. But that only made her more insecure, and the cycle continued.

Around this time, I got an unsolicited job offer from a news magazine to cover the same beat and stay in the same city. As far as magazine jobs go, it was a great offer, and it came with a raise. I really wanted to stay at the paper, but I knew that if I kept working with my current editor, there was nowhere for my career to go but down. So I met with the section editor again and told him about the magazine offer. He asked me if I wanted to leave the paper, and I said no. But I also told him that I felt I had no choice but to accept the job, because my working conditions had gotten so bad. Only then did he assign me to a new editor. A few weeks later, my former editor was transferred to another section of the paper.

Ideally, it would have been great if my boss had acted in a professional manner. When she didn't, it would have been great if her boss had been willing to get more involved with the situation, especially once it became clear that we couldn't solve the problem ourselves. In raising my concerns with both my editor and the section editor, I tried to act professionally and focus on my work and how it was suffering from this unnecessary conflict. If I had made it into a personal thing, the section editor would probably have been more reluctant to get involved. I also think that acting professionally lent more credibility to my side of the story.

If you threaten to quit too often, you can develop a reputation as a prima donna. But on the other hand, you can't go through your career with blinders on. You've got to remember that you have to look out for yourself and make the moves that are necessary to keep your career moving forward.

Visit Vault at www.vault.com for insider company profiles, expert advice, career message boards, expert resume reviews, the Vault Job Board and more.

VAULT CAREER LIBRARY   139

What if my boss is incompetent?

Do not try to cover up your boss's incompetence by trying to figure out everything on your own. If you pull it off successfully, your manager will probably take credit for your work, while his incompetence continues to go unnoticed by his superiors. If you fail, your manager could publicly blame YOUR incompetence and review you badly. Either way, you will waste a lot of your own time heading down the wrong path, reinventing the wheel and stunting your own professional development.

Create alternate resources and support for yourself. Ask other managers and your peers who work with good managers for their informal review or guidance to help you get your job done.

My boss is never around or always too busy to give me guidance.

Your best advice: Be persistent!

- Schedule a standing daily or weekly appointment, however brief, on her calendar. Make sure you have your questions organized during that time so you don't lose the slot.

- Stand by his desk until he answers your question; don't wait for him to return your call.

- Ask other managers for their informal review or guidance.

- Build relationships with other managers so your work gets recognized.

Bad Co-workers

What if I don't get along with a co-worker?

If you have a problem with someone's personality:

- Be nice to the person but minimize your interaction with him.

- If there is one specific thing the person does that you don't like, talk to him about it.

- Don't bitch about that person to others at the company.

If someone has a problem with you:

• Try to identify your behavior that triggers the bad reaction and proactively change it. You might have to ask your peers or talk to the person directly to find out the root cause. If it's something you can change and are willing to change, do it.

• Be extremely nice to the person, even if she is not being nice to you. Eventually, she will relent and treat you in a cordial manner.

• Minimize your interaction with that person. Don't hold a grudge – it is unhealthy and unproductive.

What if people take credit for my work?

Don't be shocked if others try to pawn off your work as theirs. Instead, keep good records of what you provide to whom so you can objectively show you originated the work. For example, you can re-forward your original e-mail documenting the work to the group if someone else tries to take credit – just write at the top of the e-mail, "As we discussed earlier …"

IMPORTANT: Don't be the policeman
Kristi Anderson, executive recruiter, TMP Worldwide

When you are a new hire at the bottom of the corporate ladder, don't take it upon yourself to be the office policeman when you perceive someone is doing something wrong if it has no impact on you or your work product. Keep your nose out of other people's business. If someone is behaving in a truly unethical or unpleasant manner, take the matter up with your manager or with an HR representative.

Visit Vault at **www.vault.com** for insider company profiles, expert advice, career message boards, expert resume reviews, the Vault Job Board and more.

V/\ULT CAREER LIBRARY **141**

Dealing with Uncomfortable Situations

Your sense of humor is your best weapon for dealing with uncomfortable situations. Sometimes, a humorous remark will defuse the most awkward or tense moments.

Here are some common situations you may experience and our suggestions for minimizing their effect on you:

Someone is yelling at you

If it is an unexpected crisis that is causing an otherwise rational person to vent in your direction, let the storm blow over and do not take it personally. More often than not, the person will feel bad and apologize once it is out of his system. If a client or a superior verbally abuses you repeatedly, look him straight in the eye and calmly tell the person that you will talk to him when he calms down. If he doesn't calm down, leave the room. If you set the precedent that you will accept personal and recurrent verbal abuse, it will definitely happen again.

Locker room humor

You may work in a very macho environment. This kind of work environment can be uncomfortable for anyone, regardless of gender, marital status, culture, religion or sexual orientation.

Try to draw your own personal boundaries about what you find acceptable and what you absolutely will not tolerate. Don't compromise your boundaries; you will regret it. If it's easier for you, make up excuses for your lack of participation and stick to them. "I can't drink; I'm allergic to alcohol." Whether you are male or female, think of a socially acceptable reason why you can't attend a happy hour or the strip club. "I have to meet my personal trainer," or "I'm going on a date."

Social outcast

All of your peers get together every Friday night to drink and dance at a particular club. You are never invited to go along. Now you are starting to notice that your peers are obviously closer to each other, bonded by their revelry, and you are not part of the crowd. They go to lunch together. They seem to know about each other's personal lives. You start to feel left out. How do you fix the situation?

- Organize an event you would enjoy and invite others to attend. Preferably pick an activity that you will be able to shine in.

- Try to befriend one person in the "group" instead of approaching the group as a whole.

- Just show up at the next trip. People will start including you after they see you out and about.

Culturally ignorant colleagues

At some point, your co-workers may reveal some sort of bias due to their own ignorance or lack of exposure, whether it's sexist, racist, homophobic or anti-religion. Try not to take unintentional offenses personally. And definitely do not take it upon yourself to educate co-workers on your personal politics, culture or religion. Likewise, be sensitive and avoid potentially ignorant remarks about other cultures, politics, ethnicity, looks or education.

Schoolyard bullies

In some tough work environments, adults can regress into junior high behavior for all the same reasons as schoolyard bullies: insecurities, personal problems, the desire to impress others. Some insecure individuals may single you out for aggressive teasing or unwanted attention, disguised as good-natured ribbing. How should you deal with the bullies?

- Make friends around the office to widen your support network.

- Try to "kill him with kindness" and ask about his work or background with avid interest.

- Most importantly, don't lose focus on your work. The faster you perform well, the faster you will be promoted and move on to bigger and better things.

- For the completely mature approach, take the guy aside and tell him in a calm voice that you perceive that he has a problem with you, and you would like to know why. It's worth a shot.

Visit Vault at **www.vault.com** for insider company profiles, expert advice, career message boards, expert resume reviews, the Vault Job Board and more.

VAULT CAREER LIBRARY   **143**

Office crushes

You will be working late nights and weekends with your peers. When you spend that much time with people, your professional and social outlets start to blur, and inevitably people develop crushes on each other.

When the attraction is mutual, you will feel very tempted to act on the situation. While it may be a fun distraction to carry on a flirtation in the office, it is almost never worth acting on. The aftermath of an office romance gone bad can have a very negative impact on your professional career and emotional health. You really want to maintain some distance between your work space and personal space.

When you are dealing with a crush that is unrequited, the situation is even trickier. If you like someone who is not responding, take it as a blessing that you are not going to get entwined in an office romance for all the reasons stated above. Let it go and move on. Consider the crush a fun distraction, but don't pursue a colleague, and don't tell others in the office of your interest. Most importantly, start scheduling fun activities outside of the office so you can meet real romantic prospects.

If someone is pursuing you and you are not interested, politely let him know that you believe in keeping space between your personal and professional life and you wouldn't consider dating anyone at work. This response keeps your rejection impersonal and allows the pursuer to maintain his dignity. Try as hard as possible to treat him the same as before; don't avoid him, as you might have in junior high! Keep his pursuit confidential; if he finds out you were gossiping about him, you will incur his wrath and you will look bad to your colleagues.

Maintaining Your Equilibrium

CHAPTER 12

Plan Vacations!

It's your prerogative to take personal time off. That's why vacation days and personal days are part of your work contract. You will regret it if you miss important family and friend events. And time away from the office will rejuvenate your enthusiasm for work, clarify your perspective and prevent burn out. Unfortunately, many managers, especially workaholics, expect you to avoid vacations. Don't fall for the guilt trip. Frankly, except in rare instances, you are just not that essential. You can afford to take a vacation without being fired or seeing the department collapse. There will never be a perfect time to take vacation, but you can minimize the conflicts by doing your homework.

- Plan around the schedule of your clients, managers and peers. Some managers prefer to stagger vacations in the department, while others don't mind if many people vacation at once.

- Try to wrap up projects before you go.

- Organize and label your files for third party ease of coverage.

- Distribute a list of the location of files and data pertinent to current projects to all of your teammates, and leave one taped to your computer.

- Provide a way to contact you in the event of a true emergency. It's OK to limit this contact information to one or two key people so you won't be harassed during your time away. One lawyer was called on his cell phone repeatedly during his wife's labor. In stressful situations, it's best to have a trusted gatekeeper to screen unwanted calls for you.

- If it is convenient and acceptable for you, tell your co-workers you will check voice mail once a day, or once every two days, at a specific time. It is unlikely they will leave you a voice mail, but they will feel better knowing that you'll check in. If you must have a totally work-free vacation, let it be known you won't be checking voice mail at all and don't look back.

- Leave an out-of-office voice mail and automatic e-mail reply that includes a contact who can respond to urgent matters while you're gone. Make sure your contacts know you've listed them as contacts, and debrief them on what to expect and where your files are.

• Make sure you appreciate the people who cover you in your absence, and bring small gifts for everyone back to the office.

If your manager does not want you to take a vacation, think about your priorities. Ask around to see what your co-workers have done about vacations in the past.

Take Care of Errands

Just because your boss spends the afternoon on the phone planning his vacation with his family or doing his banking doesn't mean you can openly do the same.

• Make personal calls before or after your co-workers get in, from a private conference room or unused office, or during your lunch hour when most people are out of the office and can't overhear.

• Try to lump appointments together so you can take a day off here and there to get them all done.

• Take advantage of perks in your office like dry cleaning delivery, so you don't have to do it on your own time.

• When the boss is away, the employees … run small errands. Your boss will probably not try to look for you when she is on a plane, at a business development meeting or at a personal appointment during the workday.

Pick Your Battles

Let the petty stuff go, like seating arrangements, title and office furniture. Instead, focus on learning your business, building your skills and expanding your network of contacts. Worrying about small issues saps your energy and makes you seem petty.

Take Care of Your Mental Health

Do not rely on your youth to get through this period of your life. The human body is not made to sustain prolonged periods of work without sufficient sleep, healthy food and exercise. If you are truly burning out, what do you do?

Many companies offer free counseling through their insurance for employees. Go ahead and take advantage of this free service if you feel like you're going to explode. Don't underestimate the emotional drain of work-related stress. Check with your benefits manager in the human resources department if you are not sure what your insurance covers. Don't worry, your benefits manager and your insurance carrier will keep your requests confidential.

If you want to quit, take a short vacation first. Schedule time off as soon as you can far from cell phones, e-mails and computers. During this time, think hard about what you want out of life, and what your career goals are, with a clear head.

Fantasizing about the Future as a Pick-Me-Up

Former management consultant

When your job gets you down, always know many other options are available to you. Don't think of any one experience as an end-all-be-all. There are always more choices to be made and more jobs to be had! Make a list like I did of "new opportunities," and open it every time you are feeling down.

Take Care of Your Physical Health

There is no one looking after you in an office besides you, so you must prioritize your own well-being.

See the doctor if you are sick. Typically, you get sick when you are working the hardest because you are not getting enough sleep, not exercising, not eating right and completely stressed! At these times, up against a deadline, it seems impossible to take two hours out of your day to go see a doctor. It is not worth enduring prolonged illness for your work. Get to the doctor and get medicine to help you function and feel better. And stop spreading your germs at work.

Visit Vault at **www.vault.com** for insider company profiles, expert advice, career message boards, expert resume reviews, the Vault Job Board and more.

VAULT CAREER LIBRARY   **147**

As a consultant, Patty once endured a flu that dragged on for weeks because she was working seven days a week, and felt like she couldn't spare the time to see a doctor. She started to think of her sickness as an interesting challenge to her immune system and remarked to a friend, "I haven't seen a doctor and I'm not taking any drugs at all, but I figure it's just a matter of time before my body naturally fights off the virus, right?" His response was, "Or you'll just die."

Beware of work strain on your body! Everyone who works regularly on a computer is susceptible, and the results can be permanently damaging to the flexibility, function and strength of your back, neck, shoulders, arms and hands.

- Ask your office to provide an ergonomically correct chair, mouse, mousepad, keyboard, computer desk and headset phone.

- Sit correctly. You should sit upright, your with shoulders straight and elbows at right angles. Your lower back should press against the back of the chair, and your feet should be flat on the floor.

- Type in a neutral position. Your forearms, hands and wrists should be flat.

- Your monitor should be directly in front of you, about an arm's length away, and glare-free. Your eyes should be level with the top of the screen.

- Do eye exercises to reduce eye strain. Don't forget to blink while you are staring at your computer screen. Use re-wetting eye drops. Look out the window every thirty minutes, focus on a distant landmark and trace the horizon.

- Stretch your body at least once an hour. Take a walk, do some jumping jacks, touch your toes. (You should do this outside or in a restroom.)

- If you get neck aches, get a headset. Avoid cradling the phone with your head. Exercise your neck muscles by using your right hand to tilt and hold your head to the right (gently!) for ten seconds, then switch sides. Repeat several times a day.

- If you get back and shoulder aches, do shoulder shrugs and shoulder rolls each 10 times a day slowly. Pretend you are a chicken and bring your elbows together behind your back several times a day. Also, hold one bent arm at the elbow across your chest with your other hand for 10 seconds. Repeat with other elbow.

Drink lots of water all day long. It's good for you. Plus, it will give you a reason to get up and stretch your legs walking to the bathroom every hour.

Eat well. Eating healthy is difficult when you are working long hours, but it's worth doing.

- Don't skip meals to get more work done.
- Don't let the expense account dinners go to your waistline. You may view your expense account as secondary income from your job, but avoid eating everything in sight. While it's OK to indulge once in a while, try to regularly choose light options like salad and fish, skip dessert, and take leftovers home instead of gorging yourself.
- Avoid the junk food in the company kitchen and the vending machines. Stock your office with healthier options such as fruit, granola bars and instant oatmeal.

Eat Healthy!

A consulting analyst was working around the clock for months and only eating fast food at his desk and junk food from the company kitchen. He finally saw a doctor after feeling sick for quite a while and was diagnosed with scurvy. He had deprived his body of fresh fruit and produce for so long that he'd contracted the antiquated disease that historically afflicted sailors who were at sea for months or years at a time!

Exercise is vital to both your physical and emotional health. It is just when you are busiest at work, and when it seems impossible to get out of the office, that you need the stress-relief and head-clearing effect of a good workout. Schedule it into your daily calendar. The adrenaline of exercise and the change in your environment can generate creative new ideas about your project. Even if you have a good metabolism now, you still need to exercise because your metabolism will slow down as you age. Additionally, sports are a great way to make friends with co-workers, whether it's tennis or a work-sponsored exercise class.

Don't be a martyr and work insane hours if it's not necessary. It's OK to work all night when a deadline demands it and your team is by your side to support you. But there is no need to get in the office earlier and leave later than everyone else just to prove your work ethic. In the end, you will regret the missed social activities outside of the office. The work will be there in the morning, so go home.

Visit Vault at **www.vault.com** for insider company profiles, expert advice, career message boards, expert resume reviews, the Vault Job Board and more.

VAULT CAREER LIBRARY **149**

Ask for What You Need
Marketer at a Web-based company

I was working long hours and struggling with back pain. I knew that I needed to get physical therapy, but I was nervous about asking for time off for it because I wasn't sure how the founder of my company would react. In the end, I realized it was better to be upfront and try to work out a win-win situation. I sat down with the founder, who surprised me by being accommodating. She proposed that I work part-time for a while so I could do physical therapy in the mornings. I was shocked she was so willing to help me. Sometimes I think people may not get part-time or telecommuting options in part because they haven't asked.

Stock Your Office With Vital Supplies for Your Wellness

Create the environment you need. Decorate your office with fresh flowers, your favorite art, some pictures of loved ones, a small stereo, a small water fountain or anything else that brings you serenity. Stock supplies in your office to make your long office hours more bearable:

- **Healthy snacks.** Granola bars, instant oatmeal, fruit, bottled water and juices. You'll need the late-night fuel.

- **Face wash, toothbrush, toothpaste, lotion.** Useful for all-nighters, or just a refresher.

- **Razor for guys.** Good for all-nighters and emergency shaves before impromptu meetings.

- **Spare glasses.** Wearing your contacts during your late nights six or seven days a week is very bad for your eyes. Swallow your vanity and give your eyes a break after hours.

- **Eye drops.**

- **Comfortable shoes.** Give your feet a break if you are going to be standing by the copy machine until 1 a.m.

- **Alarm clock.** If you need to catch a catnap, just make sure you don't oversleep!

- **Medicine kit.** Make sure you have a small supply of your over-the-counter basics (e.g., ibuprofen, allergy medicine, cough medicine) handy. Bring your prescription drugs to work – if you take prescription drugs at specific times during the day, you don't want to risk missing a dose because you are stuck at work.

- **Some favorite CDs.** It's comforting to play some music if you are stuck in the office all night doing brainless stuff: making copies, binding reports, faxing long documents. Just don't blast it if other people are around trying to concentrate.

Always Maintain Perspective

Schedule activities that give you perspective about what is important in life and how good you have it. Volunteer a few hours a week or a month. How many children or senior citizens do you interact with in a typical month? Or is your entire life limited to interacting with business people just like yourself? Find a not-for-profit organization that interests you and allows for flexible volunteering, in case you travel or work on weekends often.

Manage Your Time around Hobbies
In-house lawyer

When I first started working, I assumed my employer owned all my time, both my waking and non-waking hours. If the smallest assignment were due the next day, I would cancel all my non-work commitments, including ones that I'd scheduled weeks earlier.

I've always wanted to pursue writing as an alternative career, but the first few years almost everything came before it. It was only after a few years that I started incorporating it into my schedule like anything else. I took a class and, although in the beginning I missed more classes than I attended, over time, I started making sure that I made it to the class every week. As a result, I found myself becoming more efficient with my time at work.

The earlier you learn how to manage your time and multi-task, the better off you'll be. Work with your schedule to accommodate activities that make you healthy and happy.

Visit Vault at **www.vault.com** for insider company profiles, expert advice, career message boards, expert resume reviews, the Vault Job Board and more.

V/\ULT CAREER LIBRARY   **151**

Evaluating Your Job/Moving On

CHAPTER 13

Know Your Short-term and Long-term Goals

Do you want to earn money, go to grad school, or go to another company? Your goals make a difference in the way you manage your career now.

Keep a chart mapping your goals for the short term and long term, and update it every year. Your goals may change annually, and you don't need to stick to the plan, but this map helps you understand the evolution of your goals and keeps you focused on achieving them.

For example, you can make a chart listing your one-year, three-year, five-year, 10-year, and 20-year plans to the following questions:

- Where do I live?
- What am I doing?
- How much do I work?
- How much money do I make?
- How much money have I saved?
- Am I married?
- Do I have kids?

Visit Vault at **www.vault.com** for insider company profiles, expert advice, career message boards, expert resume reviews, the Vault Job Board and more.

VAULT CAREER LIBRARY   153

For example, if your goal is to buy a house in three years, then you may feel that it is OK for you to work 80 hours a week and make a lot of money for the next three years. However, if your goal is to have two kids in the next three years, then working 80 hours a week with a busy travel schedule is not a good use of your time now.

What are you doing today that moves you closer to your goals? Life is short. If you are slaving away at work, at least have reasons why you are enduring the suffering!

What's Your Vision?
Mary Cranston, chair of law firm Pillsbury Winthrop LLP

The most important thing you can do for yourself is to work on yourself – work to get a personal vision of where you want to go. Every day prioritize to move towards those goals.

Assess Your Job's Short-term Offerings

Make sure your job is at least two of these three things:

- **Well-paid.** Let's be honest, you need to pay your bills. Do you make enough money to live at or above the level of comfort you want?

- **Interesting work.** Do you like the type of work you are doing? Is this the type of company you want to be working at? If you don't even remember what you like to do, think back to what made you happy as a kid – chances are you're still interested in those things, and they'll give you ideas.

- **A learning opportunity.** It's OK to be in your low-paying job or boring industry for the short term if you are still learning something new and stimulating your intellect. Learning technical, presentation, interpersonal, political or management skills will all come in handy in future careers.

If only one of the three things is true for you – or ZERO! – you should start looking for another job.

Always Look For Your Next Job

Keep your eyes open for other career opportunities. Waiting until you are completely burnt out at your job to start a job search is never a good idea for various reasons:

- It can take several months to find good opportunities.

- If you are laid off at the same time as your peers, you may find yourself competing with others of a similar background.

- You will not interview as well when you are feeling negative about work.

- You never know when the right opportunity will cross your path.

How to constantly remain in the job hunt

- Use headhunters to your advantage. Take headhunter calls. Do not be rude – you never know when you will need their help. Be on a first-name basis with at least one trusted headhunter. Headhunters keep you up-to-date on your worth in the market.

- Be proactive in exchanging business cards with people you meet who have interesting jobs or employers.

- Keep your resume updated. You should always have a current general resume at your fingertips in case you need to toss your hat in the ring quickly for that sudden opportunity. You should also have a few alternative resumes on file tailored to different industries or positions you find most interesting.

The main sections to include in a resume are:

- Full contact info, including an e-mail address.

- Higher education degrees and alma maters.

- Chronological listing of substantial employers, types of projects and clients you have worked on, and the skills and responsibilities of each experience. Explain your job changes if possible (e.g., company shut down or was acquired).

- Honors you have received from your employers. Because interviewees often have similar education and experience, it's difficult for prospective employers to tell if someone is really good. It always helps for them to see someone objectively recognized for their work.

Visit Vault at **www.vault.com** for insider company profiles, expert advice, career message boards, expert resume reviews, the Vault Job Board and more.

VAULT CAREER LIBRARY   155

- A few personal interests for a bit of flavor. One friend put on her resume, "Triathlete, traveler, and experienced *Good Night Moon* reader," which got her more comments and return calls than anything else.

Don't...

- Fill the entire page with dense text about your accomplishments. As with all business writing, be concise. Bullet point major experiences and be comfortable with white space on the page: it allows a reader to scan your resume quickly and pick up the highlights of your experiences.

- Include anything in your resume that you are not prepared to discuss in depth in an interview. If you can't remember what you did on a project because it was so long ago, or you don't understand what you did on a project because you were just following instructions from your manager, leave it off your resume!

- Criticize your former employer in an interview.

Know What's Going On with the Company

Remember you are an at-will employee – you can be fired at any moment, and you can leave at any moment. Trust your intuition and get out if things look bad. Be alert when:

- The company has decreased revenues, is losing customers and not closing deals.

- The company is getting bad press.

- There have been layoffs or a change in executives.

- Senior executives are distracted and having lots of meetings.

But even if you think your company is in trouble, don't slack off. Retain your high work standards.

Know Your Limits

If you think your work situation is untenable, there is no shame in changing it. Just because everyone you know is doing one thing doesn't mean you should do it, too. Planning your exit strategy will give you something to look forward to. This change could be anything from transferring between departments to changing your career altogether. Do not just stay put and develop a defeatist attitude.

It's a Small World

As much as you may want to, and as much as others may deserve it, never, ever burn your bridges. Here is how to leave gracefully.

- Try not to quit your job during a work crunch. It is really bad form, and leaving on a negative note will affect the way your co-workers and managers think about you in general.

- Tell your managers first and in person, before they hear it from someone else. Thank them for the experience of working with them. Tell them you want to keep in touch. Set your departure date and stick to it.

- Tell your clients of your imminent departure, thank them for the experience of working with them, and tell them who will be taking over their support. Tell impressive clients you want to keep in touch.

- Don't gloat about leaving. You never know if you will be asking for your old job back one day, or working with these colleagues at a new company.

- Ask managers or co-workers you like if they will be your references in the future.

- Purge your computer of personal files.

- Purge your workspace of personal effects. Don't take any company property, including intellectual property like software or customer lists.

- Keep your offer letter, performance file and project lists to refresh your memory during the interviewing process. You can ask for a copy of your HR file for your records.

- Keep paper and electronic copies of useful templates to help you at your next job.

- Think about what you want to say about your departure before you leave. Whether your HR department has a formal exit interview process or you'll

Visit Vault at **www.vault.com** for insider company profiles, expert advice, career message boards, expert resume reviews, the Vault Job Board and more.

VAULT CAREER LIBRARY   **157**

face inquisitive co-workers at farewell lunches, be prepared to answer questions like why you are leaving, where you are going, how your boss was as a manager, and suggestions for your employer to better retain employees. You can decline to answer any of these questions (just say, "I'd rather not answer."). Realize that anything you say in an exit interview will probably go in your HR file.

Final Analysis

CHAPTER 14

We hope you have found some useful advice in this book. The tips are guidelines to succeeding in a generic corporate environment. Use your own judgment as to what advice is relevant to your situation and tailor accordingly.

Don't despair if you've violated our guidelines repeatedly. The tips come from personal lessons we and our friends have learned over the years, so you are in good company! It is impossible to employ all this advice at once.

Remember that almost everything is correctable. Most importantly, appreciate this exciting time in your life. You are energetic, resilient and eager to absorb as much knowledge as possible. Go out, make friends, have fun and learn!

Robin A. Ferracone is a Worldwide Partner with Mercer Human Resource Consulting. Prior to joining Mercer, she was a co-founder and chairman of SCA Consulting, a value management, performance measurement and compensation consulting firm. She began her consulting career at Booz Allen Hamilton after graduating as a Baker Scholar from Harvard Business School.

Here is her Top 10 List of "Career-Limiting Moves" that she has personally witnessed oblivious young professionals make:

10. You show up at the client meeting expecting the partner to take notes – and you don't even have pen and paper with you.

9. You miss the airplane because your alarm clock doesn't go off.

8. You get offended when a senior person challenges your thinking.

7. You decline to take the late night flight with your manager because you need to leave earlier for adequate "beauty rest." [Robin's note: not gender-specific]

6. You erroneously assume that business casual dress will do at a client meeting and consequently show up as the worst-dressed person in the room.

5. You charge an expensive dinner at a Beverly Hills restaurant after working late when you live and work in downtown Los Angeles.

---

4. You consistently submit work in which your manager (or worse, the client) finds mistakes.

3. You don't tell your manager in advance that you will miss a deadline.

2. You disappear without letting anyone know where you are going or how to contact you for more than an hour during the work day or more than a day on the weekend.

1. You tell the client that your boss personally made more money than the client's company did last year.

APPENDIX

Appendix A: Forms

Standard Letter

[Your company letterhead, address]

Date

VIA [US MAIL, FAX, COURIER, etc.]

Client Name
Client Address

    Re: Client No. ____: Name of Matter

Dear [Client Name]:

This letter is [in reference to XYZ] *or* [in response to your letter dated XYZ] *or* [in response to your request of XYZ].

If you need to reach me, please call me at [direct dial], or e-mail me at [e-mail address]. Thank you for your assistance in this matter.

Sincerely,

[Your name]

[Your title]

Enclosures. [Add this if you are enclosing anything with your letter]

Visit Vault at **www.vault.com** for insider company profiles, expert advice, career message boards, expert resume reviews, the Vault Job Board and more.

VAULT CAREER LIBRARY   **163**

Standard Memo

MEMORANDUM

To:

From:

Date:

Re:

I.   FACTS [The facts of the situation surrounding the issue]

II.   ISSUE [The issue the memo is addressing]

III.   ANALYSIS [What considerations, rules, policies are you taking into account? Apply them to your situation]

IV.   CONCLUSION [Recommendations, action items]

Standard Notes from a Meeting

Date:

Time:

Place:

Attendees:

Issues Discussed:

Action Items/Follow-up:

Visit Vault at **www.vault.com** for insider company profiles, expert advice, career message boards, expert resume reviews, the Vault Job Board and more.

VAULT CAREER LIBRARY   165

Standard Fax Cover Sheet

[Company letterhead]

Date: March 2, 2003 [set this on auto-date]

To: Client Name

Company: Client Company Name

From: Your Name

Fax:

Total pages: [This lets the recipient know if not all the pages came through]

Message:

Per your request, please see the attached.

The material transmitted herein is intended only for the named recipient. If you have received this transmission in error, or have not received the total number of pages, please contact the sender at the number given above.

About the Authors

Patricia Kao:

Patricia graduated from Stanford University in 1993 with a degree in Economics. Patty spent over four years at SCA Consulting, a boutique consulting firm in Los Angeles, where she started as a Business Analyst and then became an Associate. (SCA has since been acquired by Mercer Consulting.) Patty currently heads the Business Planning department for House of Blues Entertainment, a music company headquartered in Hollywood.

Susan Tien:

Susan graduated from Harvard College in 1993 with an A.B. in Organizational Psychology, and from University of Pennsylvania Law School in 1996 with a J.D. During the Internet boom, she worked at one of Silicon Valley's largest law firms, Wilson Sonsini Goodrich & Rosati. She next went in-house as corporate counsel to various high tech companies including Exodus Communications, eBay, and Silicon Graphics, Inc., where she currently works.

Contact them at pattyandsusan@yahoo.com

Visit Vault at **www.vault.com** for insider company profiles, expert advice, career message boards, expert resume reviews, the Vault Job Board and more.

VAULT CAREER LIBRARY   **167**

Losing sleep over your job search?
Endlessly revising your resume?
Facing a work-related dilemma?

Super-charge your career with Vault's newest career tools: Resume Reviews, Resume Writing and Career Coaching.

Vault Resume Writing

On average, a hiring manager weeds through 120 resumes for a single job opening. Let our experts write your resume from scratch to make sure it stands out.

- Start with an e-mailed history and 1- to 2-hour phone discussion
- Vault experts will create a first draft
- After feedback and discussion, Vault experts will deliver a final draft, ready for submission

Vault Resume Review

- Submit your resume online
- Receive an in-depth e-mailed critique with suggestions on revisions within TWO BUSINESS DAYS

Vault Career Coach

Whether you are facing a major career change or dealing with a workplace dilemma, our experts can help you make the most educated decision via telephone counseling sessions.

- Sessions are 45-minutes over the telephone

"I have rewritten this resume 12 times and in one review you got to the essence of what I wanted to say!"

– S.G. Atlanta, GA

"It was well worth the price! I have been struggling with this for weeks and in 48 hours you had given me the answers! I now know what I need to change."

– T.H. Pasadena,CA

"I found the coaching so helpful I made three appointments!"

– S.B. New York, NY

For more information go to
www.vault.com/careercoach

VAULT
> the most trusted name in career information™

Visit Vault at **www.vault.com** for insider company profiles, expert advice,
career message boards, expert resume reviews, the Vault Job Board and more.

VAULT CAREER LIBRARY   **169**

Use the Internet's
MOST TARGETED
job search tools.

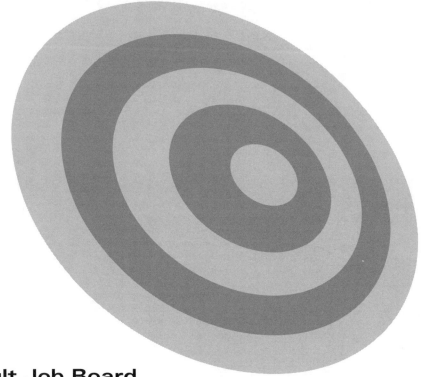

Vault Job Board

Target your search by industry, function, and experience level, and find the job openings that you want.

VaultMatch Resume Database

Vault takes match-making to the next level: post your resume and customize your search by industry, function, experience and more. We'll match job listings with your interests and criteria and e-mail them directly to your inbox.

VAULT
> the most trusted name in career information™

Visit Vault at **www.vault.com** for insider company profiles, expert advice,
career message boards, expert resume reviews, the Vault Job Board and more.

VAULT CAREER LIBRARY   **171**

Visit Vault at **www.vault.com** for insider company profiles, expert advice, career message boards, expert resume reviews, the Vault Job Board and more.

VAULT CAREER LIBRARY   **173**

Use the Internet's
MOST TARGETED
job search tools.

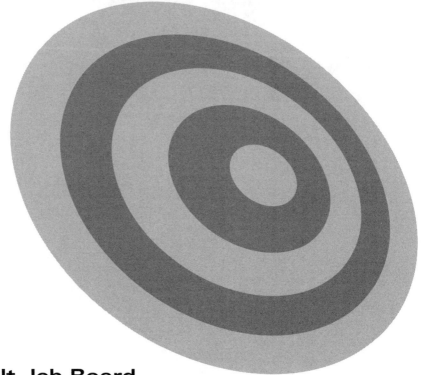

Vault Job Board

Target your search by industry, function, and experience level, and find the job openings that you want.

VaultMatch Resume Database

Vault takes match-making to the next level: post your resume and customize your search by industry, function, experience and more. We'll match job listings with your interests and criteria and e-mail them directly to your inbox.

V/\ULT
> the most trusted name in career information™

Visit Vault at **www.vault.com** for insider company profiles, expert advice, career message boards, expert resume reviews, the Vault Job Board and more.

VAULT CAREER LIBRARY   **175**